Humboldt Bay Shoreline, North Eureka to South Arcata:
A History of Cultural Influences

Humboldt State University Press

Humboldt State University Library

1 Harpst Street

Arcata, California 95521-8299

hsupress@humboldt.edu

digitalcommons.humboldt.edu/hsu_press

Cover Photo: Eureka Slough by Stock Schlueter

Cover design and layout by Maximilian Heirich

Interior layout by Maximilian Heirich

ISBN: 978-1-947112-49-0

Humboldt Bay Shoreline, North Eureka to South Arcata:
A History of Cultural Influences

Jerry Rohde

HUMBOLDT STATE
UNIVERSITY PRESS

Acknowledgements

This book originally appeared as an online report commissioned in 2020 by Hank Seemann, Deputy Director of Environmental Services, Humboldt County.

My thanks to the many people who provided help in creating the book. Hank Seemann and Aldaron Laird shared dozens of wonderful photos that provided unique and compelling views of the bayshore and adjacent sloughs. They both continually showed their concern for the future of Humboldt Bay and for the need to meet the threat of Sea Level Rise. Aldaron and Barry Evans offered authoritative answers to my numerous questions pertaining to subjects I knew little about. The document collection of the outstanding Humboldt County historian Susie Van Kirk was another invaluable resource; access to her work was provided by the HSU Library and by her son, Rob Van Kirk. Holly Harvey secured permission for me to use an important photo from the *North Coast Journal*. Jack Irvine provided rare and invaluable photos of the Jacoby Creek drainage. Steve Lazar shared his images from his extensive post card collection. Dan Mosier, creator of the California Bricks website, allowed me to use a photo of—what else?—a Eureka brick. Carly Marino, Special Collections Librarian and Archivist, arranged for me to use numerous photos from the HSU Library's collection, and James Garrison, Archivist and Collections Manager, provided the same assistance for photos from the Humboldt County Historical Society's collection. Rusty Moore, Adam Canter, and Greg Templeton responded to last-minute questions that allowed me to complete certain sections of the book. I also made use of several earlier interviews done for other projects; the interviewees were Frank J. Cerney, Ruthe McCabe Farmer, Carl Klingenspor, Lorine Hindley, Richard Philipsen, and Jennifer Renzullo. My wife, Gisela Rohde, reviewed the text, evaluated the illustrations, and, as always, provided many helpful suggestions.

At the Humboldt State University Press I am indebted to Kyle Morgan, Scholarly Communications and Digital Scholarship Librarian, for skillfully piloting my report into its new harbor as a book. Maximilian Heirlich, with great skill, created the computerized transformation of the original document into a publication of the HSU Press. Cyril Oberlander, Dean of the University Library, deserves recognition for his inspired vision of the Library becoming a publishing entity and for making that vision manifest.

To paraphrase John Donne, no researcher is an island, entire of itself, but rather is part of an archipelago of various other researchers and resources. I am thankful to have been so beneficently situated.

This report is dedicated to the memory of Don Tuttle,

a devoted historian and exemplary

Humboldt County employee.

Table of Contents

Figure 1: Time-lapse imaging of southeastern Arcata Bay (Aldaron Laird).

Summary

Water flows as if knowingly.

Wang Wei

The subject of this report is the shoreline of eastern Arcata Bay, otherwise known as northeastern Humboldt Bay, and what has happened to it during the last 170 years. The form of the report is a narrative history of the main facets of this time period and place, with each facet constituting a section of the report. This summary brings together certain generalizations that can be drawn from the narrative.

In recent times this shoreline has actually become what the word implies—a line of fixed position that separates the water of the bay from the land east of it. But before the arrival of whites in 1850 the line was a plane, an irregularly shaped but nearly flat surface that varied with the tides, which moved the water of the bay over the transition zone that we call a wetland. Then, gradually but implacably, what was fluid became fixed. The waters of the bay and its attendant sloughs were bounded by dikes or causeways and much of the wetlands became dry lands. A rich and dynamic ecosystem that had accommodated the needs of the local Wiyot Indians for centuries became a set of managed environments, each developed to meet the economic interests of the whites who had taken control of the land, leaving only small and disconnected patches of intertidal habitats. This is the story of that transition.

Figure 2: Time-lapse imaging of eastern Arcata Bay. Yellow shading shows first areas at risk from Sea Level Rise (Aldaron Laird).

The report was commissioned for two reasons. First, to help Humboldt County develop a Sea Level Rise plan for the Eureka Slough hydrographic area. Second, to document the human influence on the landforms and features along the shoreline between Eureka and Arcata; this documentation will aid in understanding the geomorphic setting and will show how human alterations may have changed natural processes and how the existing landscape may evolve with sea level rise.

Section I describes the geomorphology of the area between north Eureka and south Arcata, which contains two wetland areas divided by a ridgeline, called Brainard's Point, that once extended to the edge of the bay. To the south, Eureka Slough and its tributary sloughs were developed into an interconnected system of waterborne transportation corridors, while later much of the area was transformed by a single large reclamation project into a ranchland. To the north, two sloughs were separated by Jacoby Creek and were independent of one another, but much of this extensive wetland area was also subsumed by a solitary reclamation project. The wetlands ran inland to the base of the first mountain ridge, a condition that forced the first Eureka-Arcata road to follow a dryland course a considerable distance from the bay.

Section II provides an account of the Wiki people, the division of the Wiyot tribe that lived in proximity to Humboldt Bay. Like other Indians, they adapted themselves to the environment in which they lived, using the waterways for transportation by canoe and utilizing the foods and construction materials that were the bountiful products of Nature. Trail corridors led from their bayside winter villages to summer hunting and gathering camps in the mountains to the east, and the Wikis accordingly moved with the rhythm of the seasons. Except for the construction of redwood houses and the accoutrements of village life, the Wikis did little to change their physical environment.

Section III begins the story of changes wrought by the *diqa'* (the name for white people in the Wiyots' language), who started living near the bay in 1850. One of their first activities east of Arcata Bay was the development of transportation corridors of various types. The trees of the primeval, old-growth redwood forests east of the bayside wetlands were converted into logs, which initially were "run" down the several sloughs to Humboldt Bay, where they were towed in rafts to the bayside lumber mills. At first, the changes to most of the wetlands were incidental; the main alteration was to the streams and sloughs, which absorbed the pounding and gouging of the logs as they were washed towards the bay by fall and winter freshets. Such runs began in the 1850s and lasted until about 1880, when logging railroads started moving the logs to dumping sites far down the sloughs, whence they could be floated to the bay rather than pushed there in a tumbling mass by a sudden surge of water. Before the advent of the railroads some logging operations used gravity-propelled tramways, where trains of log cars were sent down inclines to the sloughs and, when emptied, were pulled back to their starting points by a horse or mule. The bay itself became a transportation route, used not only to tow logs to the mills, but also to take passengers on ferries, a frequently used option before the development of adequate land routes.

There developed two land-based travel corridors east of the bay. Starting in the 1850s, a primitive road ran between Eureka and Arcata through the Freshwater area, Indianola, and Bayside, skirting the eastern edge of Humboldt Bay's wetland complex and often hugging the base of the first mountain ridge. The road was gradually improved and served until the early 1900s as the only land route. Meanwhile, full-scale logging railroads, using steam locomotives, were built into the drainages of Ryan Creek, Freshwater Creek, and Jacoby Creek to bring logs and shingles down the canyons to dumping areas or wharves on Ryan Slough, Freshwater Slough, and Gannon Slough. All three lines were constructed in the 1880s. In order to cross the wetlands along the western portions of their right-of-ways, the timber companies constructed causeways for the tracks to run upon. These causeways became the first major human-made alteration to the bayside landscape, for they were, in effect, dikes that impeded the flow of water through the wetlands.

In 1901 the second travel corridor opened when the Eureka & Klamath River Railroad began running trains between Eureka and Arcata on tracks located just inland from deeper portions of the bay. Now a continuous railroad causeway that connected those two cities formed a barrier between the wetlands and the bay. From south Arcata to Brainard's Cut a second railroad causeway, a few feet closer to the bay, had been built before construction was halted when competing rail lines merged rather than run duplicate sets of tracks. Another causeway, just inland from the rail line, was built between 1918 and 1925 for what became Highway 101. In the 1950s a parallel causeway was added when the two-lane highway was converted to a four-lane freeway.

Section IV: In the 1890s two massive land-reclamation projects were initiated in the wetland areas north and east of Arcata Bay. In 1892 John Harpst and O. H. Spring diked the bay shore from Butcher's Slough to Jacoby Creek, creating grazing lands for dairy herds, including those of the Three C Ranch southwest of Sunny Brae. In 1895 Reuben and Mary Gross and John A. Sinclair used the same dredging machine to develop a dike system that ran from Freshwater Slough nearly to Brainard's Point, creating another dairy ranching area that was soon leased by the Hanson brothers.

The diking essentially created a wall between Arcata Bay and the adjacent wetlands, where the natural interflow of water was obstructed and replaced by tide gates that allowed drainage to the bay but not the return flow of tidal inundation. The land "reclaimed" by the dikes converted areas that had previously supported a wide range of plant and animal life to narrow, three-stage production systems where clover-rich grasslands fed dairy cows that then manufactured milk as the money-making final product.

Section V: Various commercial areas were developed near the eastern edge of Arcata Bay, including the Sass Tannery, Murray Field airport, the ARCO mill at Brainard, the Bracut Lumber Company at Bracut, oyster farms at Bracut, two brickyards on Eureka Slough, a drive-in theater at Indianola Road, and a string of businesses on Jacobs Avenue. All of these created changes in the Arcata Bay shoreline or in the inland sloughs and wetlands, adding their impact to those created by the railroad and highway corridors that were superimposed on the area. These businesses all required or otherwise caused alteration of the natural environment, where wetlands were paved over and built upon, waterways truncated and polluted, the bay diked and dredged, and clay-bearing soils mined to extract the resource.

Section VI: A selection of maps and photos illustrates current conditions on the sloughs and shoreline of eastern Arcata Bay. Unless someone uses a kayak or a drone they will have little opportunity to observe most of the locations covered by this part of the report. The portfolio shows features that resulted in part from actions that may have occurred a hundred years or more in the past, and which will either require alteration now or at some time in the foreseeable future due to Sea Level Rise.

Section VII: A brief concluding statement helps place this report within the ongoing responses to Sea Level Rise.

Figure 3: A partial return to the past: the Eureka Slough system in flood, 1948 (HSU Library).

Timeline of Significant Events

December 1849: The Josiah Gregg Party is led around the east side of Arcata Bay by the Wiyot Indian Ho-dar-ros-samish. Little was recorded about the trip other than it occurred on Christmas Day.

November 1850: William Carson and Jerry Whitmore cut Humboldt County's first saw log near Ryan Slough.

1853: Arnold Call Spear homesteads 160 acres just south of the Freshwater Slough wetlands, making him one of the first landowners in the area.

c. 1855: Athabascan Indians from Kneeland area attack the Wiyot fish camp *gomeododog* near Freshwater Corners.

1855: A primitive county road opens from Eureka to Arcata on a route east of the Arcata Bay wetlands.

1859: Some 600,000 board feet of timber washes down Ryan Slough in a torrential storm.

February 1860: Thirteen Wiyot survivors of the Indian Island Massacre use Eureka and Freshwater sloughs to reach safety at the Spear homestead.

1862: A revised Eureka-Arcata road uses a causeway to cut across the Freshwater wetlands in the vicinity of today's Freshwater Farms.

1864: John B. Hill starts a brickyard on the south side of Eureka Slough.

1875: McKay & Co. starts sending their logs down Ryan Slough on the way to the company's Occidental Mill in Eureka.

1875: Dolbeer & Carson build a tramway from their timberland near Jacoby Creek to Brainard's Slough.

1880: The Humboldt Logging Railway lays track through part of the Freshwater valley, ending at a log dump and wharf on lower Freshwater Slough.

1882: Flanigan, Brosnan & Co. builds a rail line from their timberlands on upper Jacoby Creek to Gannon Slough, where they build a log dump.

1883: McKay & Co. builds a railroad along part of Ryan Slough, eliminating log drives from that section of the slough.

1887: McKay & Co. extends their rail line northward to a point on Freshwater Slough just north of the eastern end of Park Street. A log dump is built next to the slough.

1889: Reuben and Mary Gross and John A. Sinclair purchase more than 1,000 acres of Swamp & Overflowed Lands in the Freshwater and Fay Slough wetlands.

1889: J. M. Sass starts a tannery about a mile west of Freshwater Corners. The gulch that runs through his property empties into Freshwater Slough, thereby providing a ready-made disposal system for the residue of the tanning process.

1891: Flanigan, Brosnan & Co. extends their rail line westward from Gannon Slough, building a wharf that eventually extends a mile and a half into the bay.

1892: John Harpst and O.H. Spring dike the Arcata Bay shoreline from Butcher's Slough to the mouth of Jacoby Creek.

1895: Harpst and Spring start a creamery, feeding their dairy cows clover grown on the reclaimed wetland.

1895: Reuben Gross purchases Harpst and Spring's diker.

1898: The diker has been busy. The Freshwater Reclamation District now has a dike running from Freshwater Slough almost to Brainard's Point, shielding 1,200 acres of reclaimed land from the fluidic fluctuations of the bay.

1899: Gross and partners lease their reclaimed land to the Hanson brothers. George Hanson builds a dairy on Walker Point. The Hanson dairy herd grazes upon the grassy surface of the former wetland.

1900: Three Ferndale dairymen lease part of Harpst and Spring's diked area and start the Three C Ranch.

1900: The California & Northern Railway uses steam shovels to cut through the ridgeline at Brainard's Point.

1901: The Eureka & Klamath River Railroad begins running trains between Arcata and Eureka on tracks located just inland from the edge of Humboldt Bay.

1902: McKay & Co. builds a shingle mill at their railroad terminus on Freshwater Slough.

1905: The Eureka and Freshwater Investment Company is formed; it takes over Gross and Sinclair's 1100-acre Freshwater-Fay slough property the following year.

1906: The Pacific Lumber Company extends the old Humboldt Logging Railroad, which it now owns, to a connection with the bay shore rail line at a location later known as Freshwater Junction.

1907: The Northwestern Pacific Railroad (NWP) incorporates, consolidates several local railroad lines, and now runs the line from Eureka to Arcata.

1907: C. E. Sacchi successfully sues the Bayside Lumber Company "for damage to land from water and driftwood resulting from a log jam on Jacoby Creek breaking dyke."

1908: The Haw Quarry Railroad carries rock from the quarry down tracks that parallel Ole Hanson Road to a wharf at the head of Fay Slough, whence barges towed by steamers take the rock to the foot of J Street in Eureka.

c. 1910: The Humboldt Clay Manufacturing Company is established on Eureka Slough by Harrison M. Mercer of Mercer, Fraser Co.

1914: Henry M. Devoy buys the Freshwater Investment Company's Freshwater-Fay slough parcel.

1918-1925: The Redwood Highway is constructed between Eureka and Arcata; it parallels the NWP's rail line.

1920: C. E. Sacchi sells his lease on the Three C Ranch for an amount worth $3,230,000 today.

1921: Henry Devoy and his son-in-law, Lee Gillogly, have a long row of eucalyptus trees planted adjacent the Redwood Highway.

1923: Aviator Dayton Murray creates an airstrip next to the Redwood Highway at the later site of Harper Ford.

c. 1926: A refuse dump is established north of Bracut on the "A. Batini Marsh," formerly known as Brainard Slough.

1933: A hard freeze devastates the Devoy eucalyptuses. They are cut down but new trunks sprout from the stumps.

1933: The Humboldt Bay Oyster Growers Association, Inc. starts operations with a six-acre oyster bed on land leased from the NWP at Brainard's Point.

c. 1933: The Batini dump closes and is replaced by a new facility on Cummings Road.

1937: Murray Field opens as a county airport; two new bridges connect it to the Redwood Highway.

1940: Brothers Herb and Glenn Fehely buy the warehouse that had belonged to the New England Fish Company. With two other partners, they start the Bracut Lumber Company on the site, which is then called "Bracut."

1941: The New England Fish Company buys out the Humboldt Bay Oyster Growers Association facility at Brainard Point.

1941: The Pacific Lumber Company removes its Freshwater railroad line.

1943: The Devoy family sells part of their ranch to Charles L. East and Dorothy N. East.

1943: The aging lift span highway bridge over Eureka Slough is replaced by a truncated Parker truss bridge.

1943: The New England Fish Company closes its Brainard operation. The oyster allotments there are declared abandoned three years later.

1947: The Easts sell a portion of the former Devoy Ranch to the Arcata Redwood Company (ARCO).

1948: Carl Johnson opens a cattle auction yard at what becomes the eastern end of Jacobs Avenue.

1951: The Midway Drive-In Theater opens at the west end of Indianola Road; its parking lot obliterates a small section of wetland.

1952: ARCO finishes building its remanufacturing mill at what becomes known as Brainard.

1952: The Bracut Lumber Company creates a 32-acre addition to its property by diking a section of the bay and infilling part of it. The company builds a conical burner, planing mill, and one other structure on the infill and begins milling lumber at the site.

1954-1957: ARCO demolishes the former ranch buildings on its site and expands its drying yard.

1955: The Michael J. Burns Freeway opens between Eureka and Arcata. The highway corridor is now four lanes wide.

1958-1960: ARCO reclaims additional parts of Humboldt Bay on the north and east sides of its parcel.

1960: Bracut Lumber begins a new dike on the bay using the dredge *Jupiter*, which builds the south arm of the dike 1,500 feet into the bay before the project is abandoned; instead the 1952 dike is gradually infilled over the subsequent decades.

1968: A retail lumber yard opens at Bracut Lumber.

1998: The Federal Railroad Administration officially closes the successor owner of the NWP.

I. The Setting

The portion of Humboldt Bay north of the city of Eureka is generally referred to as Arcata Bay or sometimes North Bay (USGS 1942, 1951, 1972). The eastern side of Arcata Bay can be divided into two distinct drainage units, or hydrographic areas. To the south is the Eureka Slough complex, which runs from that slough's mouth northeast to Brainard's Point, which, before alteration, was the western end of a low ridge that ran in an arc from the bay to the first main inland ridgeline. The Brainard ridge served as a natural drainage divide separating the Eureka Slough complex from wetland areas to the north. The northern area included, in order from south to north, Brainard Slough, Jacoby Creek, and Gannon Slough. Here the sloughs were shorter and less complex than those to the south, while Jacoby Creek was a perennial stream that emptied directly into the bay rather than into a slough.

In the Eureka Slough complex, a system of seven sloughs has defined the cultural development of the shoreline and areas immediately inland of southeastern Arcata Bay. Eureka Slough meets Arcata Bay at the extreme northeastern corner of Eureka. It extends inland for about two miles, first in a southerly and then in an easterly direction. For much of its course the slough runs nearly parallel to the bay, creating the small peninsula on which Jacobs Avenue and its business district were constructed. Along the first mile of its course, the southwestern side of Eureka Slough is fed by three small, southerly running sloughs that have substantially affected the development of eastern Eureka. These small sloughs have incised themselves on the inclined plane upon which Eureka rests, essentially isolating Myrtletown from Eureka proper and creating two narrow corridors of businesses and residences that follow the courses of West and S streets and of Harrison Street.

Figure 4: King Tide at Fay Slough (Aldaron Laird).

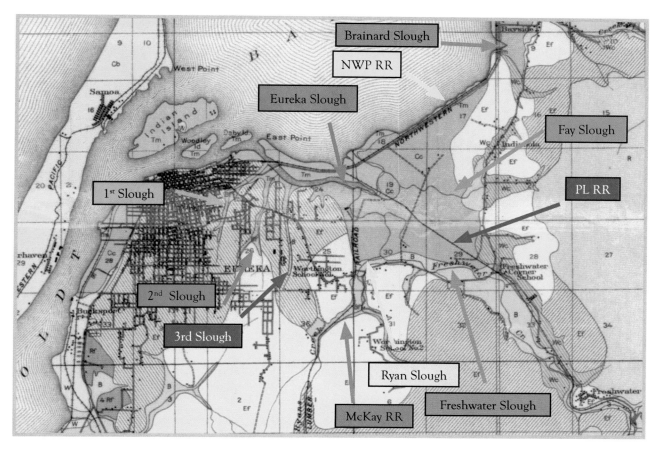

Figure 5: A 1921 base map of the southern portion of the study area, showing selected natural and cultural features (United States Department of Agriculture, Bureau of Soils 1921).

First Slough meets Eureka Slough just south of the Highway 101 bridge. It passes west of the Myrtle Grove Cemetery, leading to its nickname of Graveyard Gulch. The gulch runs just east of Eureka High School, where Albee Stadium nestles within it. It ends about one block south of Buhne Street. Second Slough, or Second Gulch, connects with Eureka Slough near the end of Bay Street. It is sometimes called McFarlan Street Gulch, after the street it parallels. It divides just north of Zane Junior High School and its two sections continue south to the vicinity of Harris Street; the dip in Harris west of Dolbeer Street is caused by one branch of the gulch. Third Slough joins Eureka Slough about one-quarter mile southeast of the end of Bay Street. It is sometimes called the Harrison Street Gulch since it runs just to the east of and parallel to Harrison Street. It ends at Harris Street a block east of Harrison Street (Jewett 1964:3).

Eureka Slough continues eastward for a mile past Third Slough. Just southwest of Murray Field it divides. One branch becomes Fay Slough, which wriggles east for a mile before ending southeast of Walker Point near Myrtle Avenue. The second branch turns south and becomes Freshwater Slough, which wends its way southward for about a mile before Ryan Slough branches off to the southwest. Freshwater Slough then bends east, running for another mile before ending near Freshwater Corners.

Figure 6: The Highway 101 corridor forms a barrier between Arcata Bay and the nearby wetlands (Humboldt County Public Works).

The 1870 Coast Survey map of the area shows six locations between the mouth of Eureka Slough and Brainard's Point where branches of either Eureka Slough or Fay Slough connected with Arcata Bay, indicating that in earlier times these slough branches created eight small islands (United States Coast Survey 1870).

Seen as a unit, the Eureka Slough system forms an extended, V-shaped wetland area, with one tip of the V at the mouth of Eureka Slough and the other tip near the Indianola Cutoff interchange. The point of the V is in the Freshwater Valley about three-quarters of a mile south of Myrtle Avenue. From this latter location the valley of Freshwater Creek extends southeasterly a mile to the town of Freshwater and then progressively divides into narrowing canyons. The 1921 Department of Agriculture soils map shows, with great beauty and precision, the overlay of cultural features that had imposed itself on the natural environment during the seven decades of white occupancy of the area (United States Department of Agriculture, Bureau of Soils 1921).

North of the Eureka Slough complex is an extended wetland area that borders all of the northern end of Arcata Bay. It includes Brainard Slough, Jacoby Creek, and Gannon Slough, the drainages of which are considered in this report. Both Brainard Slough and Gannon Slough are short in length, ending near the first inland mountain ridge, which runs about a mile back from the bay. This rid-

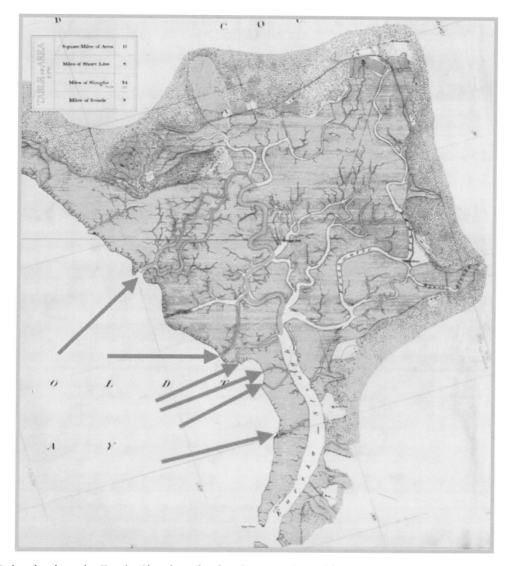

Figure 7: Eight islands in the Eureka Slough wetlands. They were formed by extensions of two sloughs. The extensions associated with Eureka Slough are outlined in pink; those with Fay Slough, blue (United States Coast Survey 1870).

geline is rent by the valley of Jacoby Creek, which, coming inland, narrows to a canyon and then reaches the creek's headwaters near Kneeland about ten miles from the bay.

Between Eureka Slough on the south and Gannon Slough on the north, the commercial and transportation needs of the whites began imprinting the landscape with cultural features in the 1850s. Two artificial corridors, running roughly south to north, developed. The first ran inland near the interface of the bayside intertidal wetlands and the first mountain ridge; it consisted of the various iterations of the Eureka-Arcata road. The second ran near the interface of the intertidal wetlands and subtidal mudflats; here was first a railroad line, followed some 15 years later by the state highway. These two linear features combined with sections of bayshore dikes to create a set of barriers between the mudflats and the wetlands.

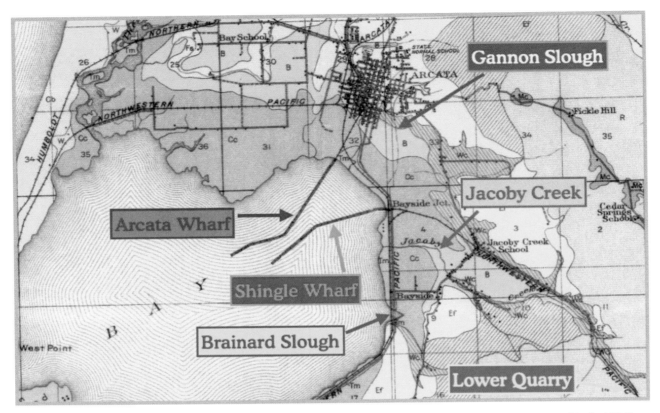

Figure 8: The northern portion of the study area (United States Department of Agriculture, Bureau of Soils 1921).

Figure 9: Northeastern Arcata Bay, with Gannon Slough (yellow arrow), Jacoby Creek (cerise arrow), and Brainard Slough (chartreuse arrow)

II. The Wiyot Presence in the Area

At the time of white arrival in 1850, Indians living near the coast from Little River to the mountains south of Ferndale spoke a common language, rendered variously by linguists and ethnographers but perhaps best reproduced as "Sulatelak" (Golla 2011:65). The language is distantly related to that of the tribe's northern neighbors, the Yuroks, and also to the Algonquian language family (Golla 2011:61-62). Sulatelak was also the name of the speakers' tribe, which was divided into three groups, each associated with a body of water.

To the north were the Patawats, who inhabited the lower Mad River (Patawat) from its mouth to just west of Blue Lake, and whose territory also extended north to Little River and south along Mad River Slough. In the center were the Wiki, who lived around the rim of Humboldt Bay (Wiki) and on Indian Island in the bay itself. On the south were the Wiyots, who occupied the Eel River (Wiyot) valley from its mouth to just north of the mouth of the Van Duzen River and whose territory also extended into the mountains south of Ferndale (Curtis 1970:226-227; Nomland and Kroeber

Figure 10: Ki-we-lah-tah, a Wiyot leader on Humboldt Bay in 1849 when he befriended the Gregg Party (HSU Library).

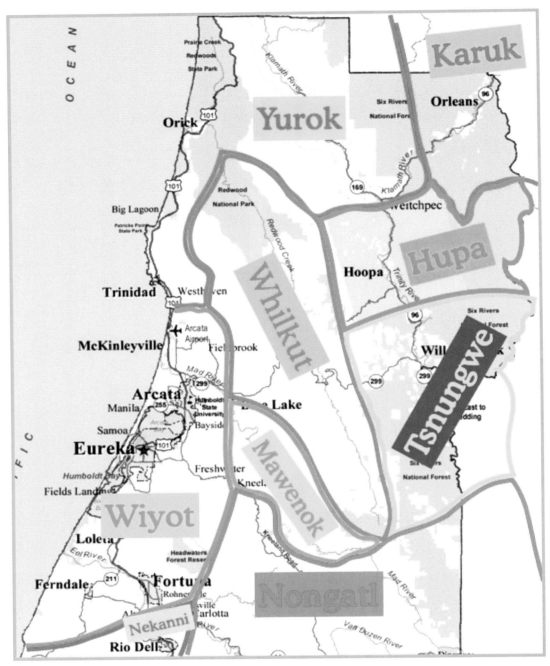

Figure 11: Tribes of Northern Humboldt County and their territories, based on published and unpublished sources. The Wiyots once bordered five other tribes (Jerry Rohde).

1936:41-44; Merriam 1976:62; Loud 1918:234, Plate 1). In time, the name of the Eel River branch of the tribe was applied to all three groups, so that the Sulatelaks came to be called the Wiyots.

The Wiyots lived in villages that were close to water, for they were people of the wetlands, where much of their sustenance came from bay, slough, or river, and where they could often travel more easily by canoe than on foot. Although the Wiyots were considered "as 'coastal' in residence as a people could be . . . they used the ocean very little for either subsistence or travel" (Nomland and

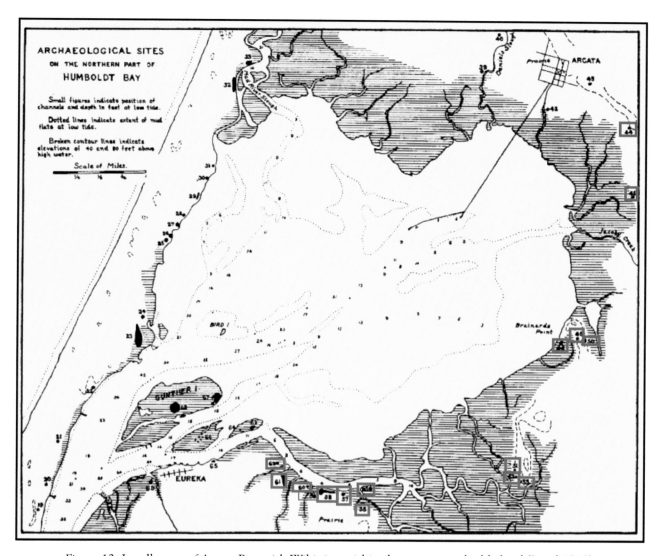

Figure 12: Loud's map of Arcata Bay, with Wiki sites within the report area highlighted (Loud 1918) .

Kroeber 1936:45). Instead of braving the high seas, the Wiki branch of the tribe centered daily life on and around the relatively placid waters of Humboldt Bay. The connection was so close that "every bay settlement was on tidewater" (Nomland and Kroeber 1936:45).

The vehicle that transported the Wikis and the other Wiyots was the dugout redwood canoe. L. L. Loud, whose *Ethnogeography and Archaeology of the Wiyot Territory* is the most complete source of information about the tribe, claimed that "a good sized canoe would be 18 feet long and 4 feet wide. It was made from a log by being hollowed out by fire." Redwood planks were used for Wiyot houses. Unlike other local tribes, the Wiyots not only placed the wall planks vertically but sometimes would arrange them horizontally (Loud 1918:232-233).

The Wikis occupied a string of villages that, like a bejeweled bracelet, encircled Humboldt Bay. Using their canoes for transportation, the Wikis traveled along about 30 miles of channels in Humboldt Bay and about 30 miles of adjacent sloughs (Loud 1918:304-305). Paddling upon these waterways they could reach their various villages and also gather numerous kinds of food. In addition, a trail system connected the Wiki villages with one another and also with the other two divisions of the tribe, Patawats to the north and the Wiyots to the south.

The main Wiyot travel route extended from the mouth of the Mad River to the mouth of the Eel, running down Mad River Slough and part of the Samoa Peninsula before crossing the bay to Indian Island. Travelers on the peninsula would shout or build a fire to attract a boatman from the island (Loud 1918:231). The route continued across the bay to the future site of Eureka, arcing down and around the southern portion of the bay to the western end of Table Bluff, and then following McNulty Slough southward to the mouth of the Eel. Two side trails, one from White's Slough (near today's College of the Redwoods) and one from Hookton Slough, forked southeast to connect with the Eel River area near Fernbridge. So it was that the Wiyots, "though they rarely slept beyond the smell of salt water, managed their lives so as to avoid more than an occasional putting to sea" (Nomland and Kroeber 1936:43, 45-47).

There was another important Wiyot trail that ran from the mouth of Mad River to "Arcata Prairie" and then around the marsh on the east side of the bay to a Wiyot village above the confluence of Ryan and Freshwater sloughs; it then continued "over the hills to the rear of Eureka" on its way to the Eel River (Loud 1918:231, Plate 1).

Figure 13: Site of village of *ikatchipi*, light area in center; Eureka Slough in background, left (Loud 1918).

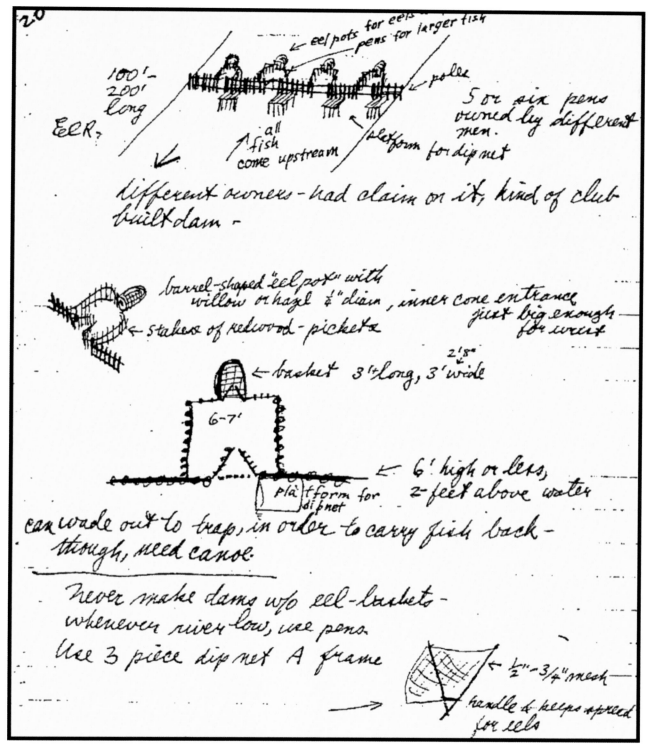

Figure 14: The Wiyots would seasonally ("June or earlier") build an intricate barrier on the Eel River designed to catch both eels (in baskets) and salmon and steelhead (using dip nets at night). Similar systems were probably used on the Mad River, Elk River, and other large waterways, including the Eureka Slough system (Hewes 1940:19-21). Such constructions probably represented the Wiyots' highest level of manipulation of their environment. Unlike the diqa' (white people) the Wiyots built permeable dams designed to hold back fish rather than water. Note that a "kind of club" of several Wiyots built each dam, although "different owners" each claimed part of the bounty that the communal dams collected.

At least three Wiyot trails connected the eastern side of Arcata Bay with inland areas. One route went from Jacoby Creek over the Fickle Hill ridgeline to the Mad River in the vicinity of Blue Lake. A second route also started on Jacoby Creek and climbed to the Fickle Hill ridge, upon which it ran southeasterly to reach Boynton Prairie. The third trail started near the head of Freshwater Slough, at the fishing camp of *gomeododog*, and then ascended eastward to Kneeland Prairie (Loud 1918:231). Travel along the latter two trails was the Wiyot equivalent of going on a sort of combination vacation and shopping trip. Instead of picking up groceries at a nearby supermarket, the Wiyots hunted and gathered in a variety of locations, both close to the coast and on the inland prairies. Among the edible flower bulbs they harvested were the so-called "Indian potato," or harvest Brodiaea (*Brodiaea coronaria*), which was found on Lindsay Creek, near Fieldbrook (Loud 1918:232, 234), and the blue, or common, camas (*Camassia quamash* ssp. *breviflora*), which grew at several locations near the coast but was also found on Kneeland Prairie (Rohde 1995; Canter 2020; Magno and Monroe 2020). The Wiyots' most important plant food grew inland, for it was the acorn of the tanoak (*Notholithocarpus densiflorus*), which was preferred above true oak acorns and was a dietary staple of many California Indians tribes (Bowcutt 2015:22-25). Forays by Wiyots from *gomeododog* into the Kneeland area were fraught with danger, since the territory was also claimed by Athabascans from the Mawenok and Nongatl tribes, who would attack Indians they considered trespassers. The photographer Edward S. Curtis described the difficulties:

> . . . the commonest cause of these affrays is said to have been the killing of Wiyot women harvesting tan-bark acorns in the mountains: for the Athapascans regarded the oak groves as their own particular property. Then the Wiyot from the bay and the rivers would unite in a war-party, and just before dawn would attack some Athapascan village, endeavoring to set fire to the houses and shoot the inhabitants as they fled. Scalps were not taken, and the Wiyot slain were brought home for burial if possible (Curtis 1970:(13):67-68).

In about 1855 the Mawenoks and Nongatls staged a retaliatory attack, coming down from Kneeland Prairie and nearby Lawrence Creek to attack *gomeododog*, which, according to the Wiyots, resulted in the deaths of two of the attackers (Loud 1918:255).

On the eastern side of Arcata Bay were several Wiyot villages or camps in addition to the aforementioned *gomeododog*. Near Bracut, where Brainard's Point once curved out to the bay, there was a village known as *plets-wok*, which meant "rock-at," along with two other earlier village sites. On Walker Point, near Fay Slough, were three village sites. At the north end of Myrtletown, next to Eureka Slough, was the village of *ikatchipi*. At least seven other Wiyot use sites were located a short distance south of Eureka Slough, all but one of which were on higher ground above the wetlands (Loud 1918:Plate 1).

From these locations the Wikis were able to easily gather the bounty of the bay and its adjacent wetlands. The black huckleberry (*Vaccinium ovatum*) was a favorite fruit; when in season the Wikis "established camps to gather it on the North Spit, where the plant developed to greatest perfection." Sweet anise (*Carum kelloggii*) was abundant on Arcata Prairie; after removing the skins, its stalks were eaten, staining the eater's lips black (Loud 1918:233-234). Salmon and other fishes were readily available. Loud, speaking about the entire tribe, indicated that "the Wiyot were preëminently a

Figure 15: After an intentional dike breach, a wetland returns near Walker Point. Wikis from three villages
lived nearby (Aldaron Laird).

fisher folk." One Indian from Blue Lake reported that "at the little sloughs near Arcata you could get
salmon with pitch-forks and fork them on the bank." Among the mollusks, the hard-shelled clam or
rock cockle (*Paphia staminea*) was probably the most abundant, but another dozen species were also
eaten. On Eel River and probably elsewhere, Wiyots built sets of multiple fish dams and eel traps
more than a hundred feet wide (Hewes 1940:20). Waterfowl were plentiful, including ducks, geese,
and mud hens (Loud 1918:237-239). The Wiyots on Eel River used an especially ingenious method
for catching geese. First they built a fire on the prow of their canoes and covered it with a sort of box
that had slits cut in it. The firelight emitted through the slits would blind the geese when the canoe
approached. Then, a lone hunter cast a flat net attached to a frame, about eight feet square, with
stone sinkers attached. Using this method a single Wiyot could catch "hundreds [of geese] . . . with
one such outfit in a single night." The haul would be divided communally (Driver 1939:375). With
such an abundance of waterfowl and fish, the Wiyots probably consumed fewer mammals than other
tribes, but Roosevelt elk and black-tailed deer were sometimes eaten, along with Pacific harbor seal,
Stellar sea-lion, and sea-otter (Loud 1918:235).

In December 1849 a group of eight whites (subsequently known as the Gregg Party), traveled from the North Fork Trinity River to the coast in search of Humboldt Bay. After many arduous adventures they camped on the Samoa Peninsula opposite the future site of Bucksport. Thwarted by the bay's entrance from continuing south, they were led by a friendly Wiki, Ho-dar-ros-samish (the father of later Wiyot leader Jerry James), around the northern end of the bay. The party camped at the future site of Arcata, *gudini*, where they celebrated Christmas by eating an elk's head they had roasted in campfire ashes. Thus fortified, they followed Ho-dar-ros-samish down the eastern side of the Arcata Bay wetlands and reached the village of *ikatchipi*, which was located on Eureka Slough in the vicinity of the later-day brickyards. From there they continued south, eventually (except for Gregg, who died along the way) bringing word to San Francisco of the "rediscovered" Humboldt Bay, thereby setting off a springtime stampede of ships filled with scores of whites eager to make the bay the supply port for the inland mines (Loud 1918:49, 248, 269, 289, Plate 1; Lewis 1966:111-170).

The seeds of hospitality planted by Ho-dar-ros-samish and other helpful Wiyots soon bore bitter fruit. By May of 1850 shiploads of the white people that the Wiyots called *diqa'* had debarked on the shores of Humboldt Bay and promptly began driving off and killing the Wiyots in order to claim their land (Rohde 2020a).

Many incidents went unreported, but in 1858 two attacks on Wiyots in the Eureka-Freshwater slough area made the news. L. L. Loud described the first event, which occurred in June:

> . . . a Mr. Knight, a lumberman, [was] living on Freshwater creek with a Wiyot woman. A Redwood Creek Indian, shooting at him and missing him, he [Knight] went to some lumbermen friends of the same disposition as himself and with them made up a story to get an excuse for killing certain Indians whom they disliked. Captain Jim and San Francisco John were accused of having done the shooting, and a very ragged hole in the hat of Knight was, in the minds of the predetermined lumbermen, sufficient proof of the guilt of these Indians. Captain Jim . . . was living at . . . [*ikatchipi*], drying fish. Knight's squaw cried and said that her people had nothing to do with the shooting, but that it was a redwood [Whilkut] Indian. However, the whites would not listen to her pleading but attacked . . . [*ikatchipi*]. They killed Nicodamus, wounded Billy in the leg, and frightfully crippled San Francisco John with three or four bullets which broke his arm and jaw and pierced his side (Loud 1918:328).

In the aftermath of this attack the wounded Indians fled to another village, while several other Indians were taken to jail. The latter were incarcerated

> . . . for a time, but as nothing could be proved against them they were dismissed. Since it would have been a flagrant miscarriage of justice for a white man's court, supported by white man's taxes, to convict a white man of any crime against an Indian, all the murderers . . . were set at liberty (Loud 1918:328).

The second attack took place in early August, when "two Indian boys were driving a train of mules from Kneeland's Prairie to Eureka." They had reached the Freshwater Corners area when "one of the boys was shot dead from his horse." The other boy, dodging the gunfire, rode into Eureka and reported the shooting, which he said was done by white men. At first no one believed him, but finally a group rode out to the scene and found the Indian's body, riddled with bullets. Apparently nothing was done to catch the culprits, but, as author A. J. Bledsoe dismissively concluded, "such cold-blooded deeds of murder . . . were condemned by all good citizens" (Bledsoe 1885:235).

Figures 16 & 17: Gravestones for Nancy and Matilda Spear at the Spear Family Cemetery, Freshwater (Jerry Rohde).

In 1853 Arnold Call Spear homesteaded 160 acres about halfway between later-day Freshwater Corners and Freshwater. He met a Wiyot woman, Matilda James, when she came to his ranch with some other Indians "to trade fresh fish for vegetables" (Davis 1977). Spear married Matilda, and they had five children. The oldest was George Spear, born in 1854 (Van Kirk n.d.). Matilda's cousin, Nancy Shakespeare, was purchased from her father by James Sykes. She was 13 when the Sykeses' son, William, was born. Within three years Nancy was in a relationship with Alburtus Hitchcock. Their first child, Andrew Jackson Hitchcock, was born in 1859. A second son, Stephen, arrived the following year (Davis 1977).

On the night of February 25, 1860, Matilda and Nancy, along with their children—George, William, Andrew, and Stephen—were at the village of Tuluwat, on Indian Island, where a Wiyot ceremonial dance had just been held. The cousins were tending to the youngest child, Stephen, who was ill. Early the next morning the women saw several white men approaching, and "they gave the alarm but it wasn't enough." The cousins and their children "ran to hide on the west side of the island." The whites massacred nearly everyone else in Tuluwat village. Afterwards, Matilda and Nancy located seven other children who were still alive. The women found "the only remaining canoe," put the eleven children in it, and "swam their way across the bay to Freshwater Creek and then walked to Matilda's husband's homestead in Freshwater" (Hunt 1998; Spear Memorial Foundation n.d.; Rohde 2020b).

So it was that the Freshwater Slough area became a landmark in the story of the survival of the Wiyot people.

III. The Development of Transportation Corridors

A. Waterborne Transport on the Sloughs

Over the centuries the Wiyot Indians used Humboldt Bay and its adjacent sloughs to transport themselves and their goods to their various villages and use areas. For a time the whites, as they developed their more elaborate transportation infrastructure, also used these waterways as conveyances. Three of the subsidiary sloughs that fed into Eureka Slough served for a time as transportation corridors.

The watersheds that fed into the Eureka Slough system were rich in redwoods, and for decades lumbermen used the creeks and sloughs to move their logs to the bay and then to their bayside mills. The method was illustrated in an 1893 promotional publication that showed rows of redwood logs "dumped into Elk River, awaiting a winter freshet" (Eddy 1893:46). The first heavy rainfall would

Figure 18: Logs gathered in the bed of Elk River awaiting rainfall sufficient to move them down to Humboldt Bay (Eddy 1893).

wash the logs down the rising river and into Humboldt Bay on the first part of their waterborne journey to the mills.

In April 1880 the *Times* carried a letter from a rancher who had encountered the effects of such log drives. Bartlin Glatt wrote that he had purchased farmland on Elk River four years earlier, when the riverbank on his property was sixteen feet high. After four seasons of log transport past his place, the banging and slamming of the huge sections of redwood had filled the riverbed with so much sediment that Glatt's bank height had been reduced to a mere nine feet (Humboldt Times, April 4, 1880). Glatt did not complete the computation, but if the rate of sedimentation remained steady, Elk River would have been sloshing over the top of its former bank in less than six years. With the same type of log transportation in effect, Ryan Slough and Freshwater Slough almost certainly suffered a similar fate.

1. Ryan Slough

It is not clear when logs were first sent down Ryan Slough, although it likely happened no later than 1853, when mill owners James T. Ryan and James R. Duff purchased land there (Rohde 2014a:1-2). Future lumber baron William Carson and associate Jerry Whitmore "cut the first tree [probably a spruce] for a saw log that was ever felled in Humboldt County" in November 1850 somewhere between Ryan Slough and the Freshwater area (Irvine 1915:608). The log may have been floated down Ryan Slough on the first stage of it waterborne trip to one of the mills in Eureka.

Figure 19: Ryan Slough, diked on both banks, just south of Myrtle Avenue (Aldaron Laird).

Figure 20: Ryan Slough north of Myrtle Avenue (Aldaron Laird).

In early 1859, when "terrible gales blew from the South-east and torrents of rain fell," on Ryan Slough "six hundred thousand [board] feet of sawlogs . . . went adrift, all the booms being insufficient to hold them against the boisterous current that swept down from the mountains" (Bledsoe 1885:273). In more placid times John McCready reportedly floated logs down Ryan Slough between about 1862 and 1880 (Irvine 1915:259), while Frank Graham, a well-known early day lumberman, recalled rafting logs there in 1872-1873 for future McKay & Co. partner Harris Connick (Irvine 1915:199).

McKay & Co., which began cutting in the Ryan Slough drainage in 1875, at first used the full length of Ryan Slough for the initial stage of their waterborne log transport, with the logs then continuing their journey on Freshwater Slough, Eureka Slough, and Humboldt Bay to reach the Occidental Mill in northwestern Eureka.

Then, progress. In 1883 McKay & Co. changed their log transport system by building a rail line next to part of Ryan Slough. At first the tracks went from Myrtle Avenue two miles upstream, with a landing at Myrtle Avenue where the logs were dumped into the slough. In 1887 the line was extended northward to a log dump a short distance north of Park Street, where the logs then went into Freshwater Slough. As before, they next traveled into Eureka Slough and were eventually towed along the Humboldt Bay shoreline to the bayside log pond of the Occidental Mill (Rohde 2014a:3-4). Thus McKay & Company finally spared Ryan Slough from the rigors of future log drives.

The rigors had been extensive; in March 1879 the *Daily Humboldt Times* noted that both "Freshwater and Ryan's slough were running full and logs were coming down lively at last reports" (Daily Humboldt Times, March 5, 1879). And in December 1881 the same paper indicated that a post-Christmas freshet washed logs down various stream courses: "about 3,000,000 [board] feet came down Ryan's Slough (Daily Humboldt Times, December 29, 1881). By 1883, however, such exciting events had been quashed by McKay & Company's new railroad.

2. Freshwater Slough

As with Ryan Slough, Freshwater Slough also became an early log transportation corridor. In November of 1860 the *Humboldt Times* reported that

> The heavy rains the forepart of the week raised the small streams putting into the Bay so as to enable the lumbermen to do a good business in "running logs." On Fresh Water slough about a million [board] feet were started from points high up and run to tide water. Another small freshet will bring down over two million feet from that stream alone (Humboldt Times, November 17, 1860).

Over the next two decades the local papers continued to document runs of up to 40,000,000 board feet of logs into the bay. Such free transportation had its drawbacks, however. Besides the erosional

186 A logging train hauling a California big tree to the Mill

Figure 21: Excelsior Redwood Company train with logs to be dumped in Freshwater Slough (thehumboldtproject.org).

effects of huge logs scraping sediment from the river channel, the timing and amplitude of the necessary freshets were inconsistent, so that in dry years the logs remained mired in the riverbeds or sloughs, creating a shortage at the mills that sometimes forced their temporary closure (Van Kirk 2006b:12).

In 1880 the *Humboldt Times* reported that this problem was being solved by a transportation transition then occurring on Freshwater Slough. The article, alluding to the god Jupiter in the guise of Pluvius, "sender of rain," noted that:

> Considerable logging has been done on this stream in years past, the logs being cut, dumped into the river and there allowed to remain until such a time as old Pluvius opened his flood gates and furnished water sufficient to float the logs down to tide water, where they could be arranged in rafts and then towed down to the mills to be cut up into lumber. But this course was necessarily slow and expensive, and if the aforesaid Pluvius was anyway sparing of his dispensation the logs would remain in the stream for two and perhaps three years. The same rule applies to the various streams used for logging purposes adjacent to the bay. The consequences would be in the time of a mild Winter the supply of logs would run short, the mills would have to shut down and the manufacturer lose large amounts of money occasioned by the delay (Humboldt Times, July 4, 1880).

The answer to this problem was, according to the *Times*, to build a railroad. Which was exactly what was happening in the Freshwater valley, where a six-mile line was under construction. The new railroad was expected to be operating in about a week, so that the caprices of Pluvius would no longer frustrate the lumbermen (Humboldt Times, July 4, 1880). Freshwater Slough thus received partial protection from the destruction wrought by log drives as the Humboldt Logging Railway laid

Figure 22: The public watches the dumping of logs into Freshwater Slough (HSU Library)

Figure 23: A steamer, probably the *Annie*, brings guests of CRC co-owner David Evans to the Freshwater Slough landing. The Myrtletown area is visible in upper left background (HSU Library)

track in the Freshwater Valley (Carranco and Sorensen 1983:121-122). However, the line terminated at a log dump adjacent the lower part of the slough (Forbes 1886), so the logs still had some distance in which to damage the waterways. In 1882 the *Times* described the log dump, or "landing":

> The "landing" is the point on the slough where the logs are rolled from the cars into the water, whence they are rafted to the mills in this city. The "landing" is made by heavily piling the bank of the slough and running an incline of logs from the height of the cars toward the water. The track runs close alongside this landing, and the huge logs are rolled from the flat cars upon the incline, from which they shoot into the water below followed by a great splash and commotion (Weekly Humboldt Times, April 22, 1882).

By 1884 (if not sooner) the landing had expanded to become a two-way operation. The California Redwood Company (CRC) sent its steamer *Annie* up to what was called Freshwater Landing, which now included a wharf, to bring supplies to the CRC's six Freshwater logging camps. The *Annie* made "daily, or at least tri-weekly trips." The landing promised to be even busier in the future, for "a new branch road one-half mile in length, a new landing, a branch road one-third of a mile long to the new shingle mill, and another from the shingle mill switch" were all either completed or under

construction. The CRC's Freshwater operation was extensive; it required the use of four steam locomotives, twenty steam donkeys, "350 white laborers and about 100 Chinamen (the latter in railroad
grading)" (Daily Times-Telephone, June 3, 1884).

The CRC's new shingle mill was to have "great capacity." It was fed by the redwood forests farther
up the Freshwater valley, where, in the first five months of 1884 some "5000 cords of shingle bolts . . .
[had] been got out by the company" (Daily Times-Telephone, June 3, 1884). By December it was reported that "the Redwood Company's shingle mill at the terminus of the Freshwater [Rail] Road is at work
and will probably continue to run all winter" (Weekly Time-Telephone, December 18, 1884). After the
Excelsior Lumber Company took over the California Redwood Company's operations, Ole Hanson

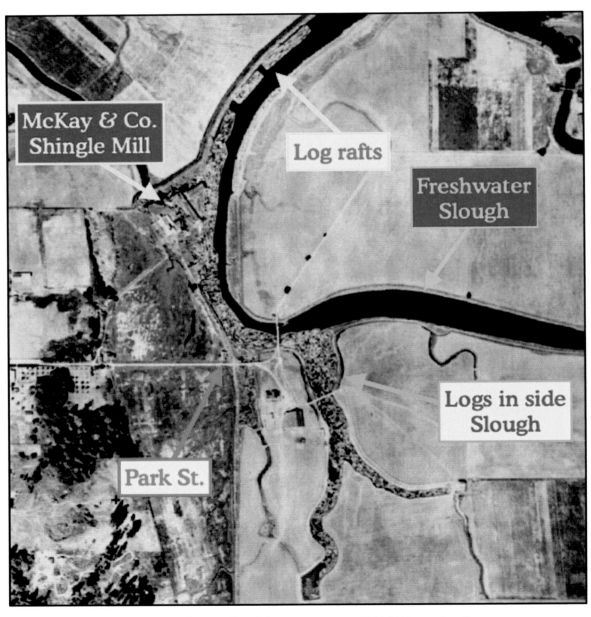

Figure 24: Freshwater Slough log storage areas, 1931 (Aldaron Laird).

Figure 25: Freshwater Slough, showing former log storage area on stub slough (Humboldt County Public Works).

was "selected as foreman" of their shingle mill in April 1886 (Daily times-Telephone, April 24, 1886). Two years later the mill was "running night and day" (Weekly Humboldt Standard, April 26, 1888).

By 1890 Hansen had his own shingle mill, turning out 50,000 shingles a day (Weekly Humboldt Standard, March 27, 1890). It was located "on the Arcata road, near Walker's Point." Hanson's mill was running "full blast" in March 1891 (Weekly Humboldt Standard, March 26, 1891) and by August it was "now on the telephone circuit" (Weekly Humboldt Standard, August 13, 1891).

In the early 1900s the Pinkerton Shingle Mill was operating in Cloney Gulch, about a mile southeast of the town of Freshwater. It cut both shakes and shingles and also "turned out red and yellow fir logs for the Bendixsen Shipbuilding Company at Fairhaven. . . ." A spur track connected the mill with the Excelsior Redwood Company's rail line on Freshwater Creek. A locomotive delivered empty flatcars to the mill, went downcanyon to do other work, and then returned to pick up the shingles and other mill products. The train then went to Freshwater Slough,

> . . . where the bundles would be 'shot' down a wooden chute to the deck of Captain Morgensen's lighter and neatly piled on wooden pallets. . . .
>
> Morgensen would then tow the lighter with his shallow-draught tug at high tide down Freshwater Slough to the Eureka Slough and on down and across Humboldt Bay to Samoa. There the load would be transferred to one the Hammond Lumber Company's steam schooners for further shipment to San Francisco . . . (Roscoe 1995:14-15).

Figure 26: High Tide on Freshwater Slough offers this Myrtle Avenue property the chance to have a boat launch (Aldaron Laird).

Figure 27: Upper Freshwater Slough in springtime, verdantly awaiting a visit by canoe or kayak (Aldaron Laird).

In later days Freshwater Slough served as a log storage area, with rafts of logs formed just downstream from the McKay & Co. shingle mill. A stub of slough near the east end of Park Street was also filled with logs that awaited rafting. The sloughs essentially served as free storage areas that allowed timber companies to build up inventory that awaited transport to the mills.

3. Fay Slough

The Fay brothers, Nahum and George M., had a shingle mill at the east end of what is now Redmond Road. According to Bert Pettingill, who worked there, the shingles were transported by a "horse tramway from the mill to deep water on Fay Slough, a distance of two miles, where they trucked the shingles and shakes for reshipment to Eureka." The tramway came down the canyon to the south of where Redmond Road was built, then turned northwest and ran a quarter-mile before crossing the Eureka-Arcata road. It continued northwest to Fay Slough, reaching it in the northeast quarter of the southwest quarter of Section 20, approximately due south of the southern end of Walker Point. There was a wharf and shed at this location, which was called Fay's Landing (Van Kirk 2007a:14-15; Pettengill 1961:3). In January 1896, as the steamer *Ruth* was towing a scow up Fay Slough

> . . . a heavy wind blew the scow upon the mud and the steamer was unable to pull it off. When the tide went out the scow careened and when high water came again it was swamped. The scow was loaded with the new machinery for the Fay mill and it is feared that it may be damaged or lost (Daily Humboldt Standard, January 18, 1896).

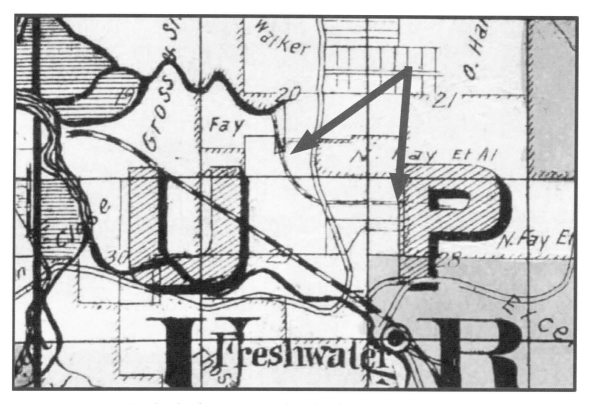

Figure 28: Route of Fay brothers' tramway from their shingle mill to Fay Slough, 1898 (Lentell 1898).

Figure 29: Tide gate on Fay Slough (Aldaron Laird).

Figure 30: Lower Fay Slough (Aldaron Laird).

For a time the Fay brothers also quarried rock on their property east of the Eureka-Arcata road (Van Kirk 2007a:16). They almost certainly transported the rock via their wharf on Fay Slough, but no report confirming this has been located.

4. Eureka Slough

Eureka Slough received not only the waters of Ryan Slough, Freshwater Slough, and Fay Slough but also the cargoes carried by these three upstream sloughs. Barges would load at Fay Slough or Freshwater Slough with quarried rock or shingles, while logs would be floated down Freshwater Slough or Ryan Slough. Sooner or later all of the traffic reached Eureka Slough, which then carried whatever was upon its surface to Humboldt Bay. From there the routes led south, whether to the South Jetty, the City of Eureka's rock bunkers, or the bayside pond of one of several lumber mills.

The Thompson Brick Company, whose operation was on the south side of Eureka Slough, used a wharf on the slough to load their bricks for transport (Dietrich 1928:81). In later days, logs were

Figure 31: May Pearsall on Eureka Slough, c. 1910 (author's collection).

Figure 32: Murray Field area, 1947, showing log booms and rafts on Eureka Slough (HSU Library).

Figure 33: Tide gate near eastern end of Eureka Slough (Aldaron Laird).

corralled by booms on upper Eureka Slough, opposite Murray Field, and were then towed down the slough for use by the Arrow Mill, at the foot of J Street in Eureka, and other mills (Rohde n.d.).

5. Brainard Slough

Early maps show a large body of water just north of Brainard's Point and a short distance east of the bay. The amended 1890 Surveyor General's map of the area designates the location as "Swamp & Overflowed Land," with a location a short distance southwest of the modern-day junction of Bayside Cutoff and Old Arcata Road being designated "Slough" (U. S. Surveyor General's Office 1890a). The slough area was fed by two streams, Rocky Gulch from the southeast and Washington Gulch from the northeast. The slough was seldom referred to by name, perhaps because at an early date it was more or less altered out of existence.

The cause of the alteration was the Dolbeer & Carson Lumber Company, which owned the forest land east of the slough. In the 1870s Dolbeer and Carson acquired the Henry Washington claim south of Jacoby Creek (Carranco and Sorensen 1988:93). In February 1875 "a reliable authority" indicated that

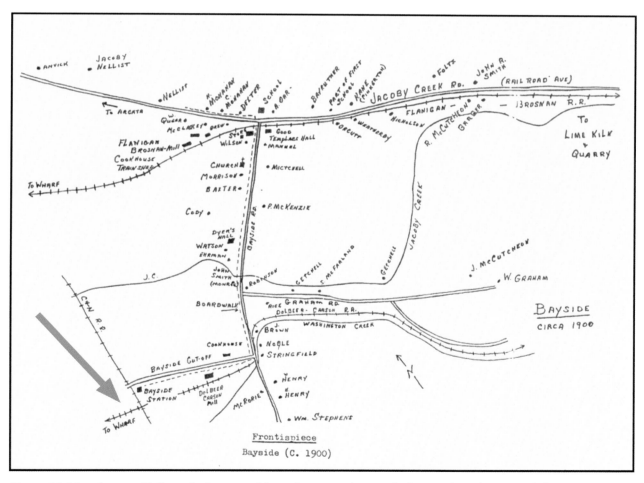

Figure 34: Map showing Dolbeer & Carson rail line after its tracks were laid on a wharf that extended into Arcata Bay (Schafran 1984).

Dolbeer & Carson will build a railroad with iron tracks from their timber possessions on Jacoby creek to the old dump of the "Washington" claim near the Eureka and Arcata road. The [rail]road will be a mile and a half long (West Coast Signal, February 17, 1875).

Perhaps there was an earlier rail line at this location, since the 1870 Coast Survey map shows tracks running southwest to cross what is now called Old Arcata Road and then ending at the northeastern tip of a feeder stream of Brainard's Slough (United States Coast Survey 1870). Or perhaps the newspaper account referred to an upgrade of an existing tramway that was to now to use "steel tracks."

A retrospective account of the Dolbeer & Carson rail line (D&C) states that on the south side of Jacoby Creek

> . . . the Carsons [sic] had a little railroad . . . that ran down to the creek, then turned toward Brainard. The logs were hauled to the slough that ran past the old Eureka garbage dump, near Brainard, and then on up into Baumgartner's pasture. The railbed ended there beside the slough with a log dump. The logs were towed out to Humboldt Bay at high tide and on to the Carson Mill at Eureka's waterfront" (Fountain 2001:(50)171).

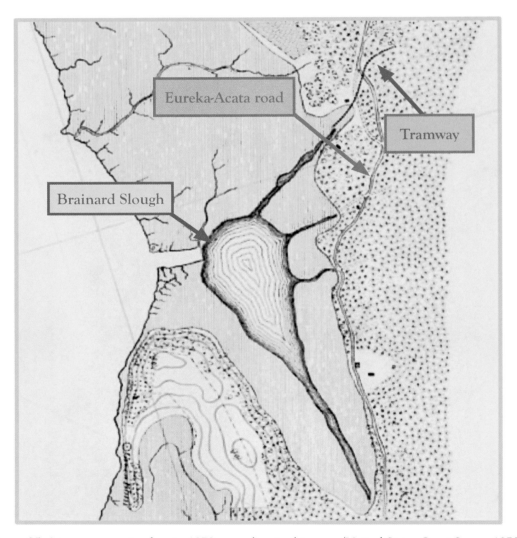

Figure 35: A tramway was in place in 1870, according to this map (United States Coast Survey 1870).

Figure 36: Remnants of the Dolbeer & Carson log transport system in 1948 (HSU Library).

H. Baumgartner owned a parcel of land just south of Bayside Cutoff and just west of Old Arcata Road. The "Eureka garbage dump" was just south of the exit point of the slough (Metsker 1949:33)

According to an anonymous account, the slough was converted into a Dolbeer and Carson log pond by damming its mouth:

> The Carson road was at first a gravity line and it was possible to run the loaded cars to the terminal without locomotive power (and then pull them back to the woods with horses). In 1881 2 million [board] feet of logs were carried in this manner from the woods to the pond formed by damming the slough near Brainard's Point. From the pond the logs were run into the bay and then rafted to the mill at Eureka (Fountain 2001:(50)294).

An 1881 account describes the "Jacoby Creek Railroad," as being under construction by Dolbeer and Carson. It was "to be extended from tide-water up into the forest. . . . The loaded cars will reach tide-water by their own momentum; horses are then used to return the cars to the upper end of the road" (Elliott 1881:139). The system was expanded when "[a] small locomotive was later brought in to help bring the logs to tidewater" (Carranco and Sorensen 1988:94).

None of the above accounts indicates that the D&C went any closer to the bay than "tidewater," a term that could possibly include the arm of Brainard Slough where the end of the rail line was mapped in 1870. Two later maps, however, show that the D&C rail line eventually went all the way to Humboldt Bay. Walter Schafran, mapping "Bayside circa 1900," shows the rail line continuing west past the "Dolbeer Carson [Shingle] Mill," crossing the C&N tracks, and continuing on "to wharf." Schafran indicates that Dolbeer and Carson built the wharf but does not give a date (Schafran 1984). Railroad historian Stanley Borden draws a vague arc for the rail line, with its western terminus a short distance out into Humboldt Bay (Borden 1958:2). Both the 1933 and 1942 USGS quads show a wharf projecting into the bay at the mouth of Brainard Slough (USGS 1933, 1942). It is probable that the wharf was used for transporting the shingles that Dolbeer and Carson cut at their nearby mill, while their logs were floated from their pond out into the bay, made up into rafts, and then towed down what was called Brainard Channel (Arcata Union, March 31, 1894) to their mill in northeastern Eureka. As mentioned below, Flanigan, Brosnan and Company used a similar division of transportation west of Bayside, where their logs were dumped into Gannon Slough and their shingles taken out onto their wharf.

The Dolbeer & Carson logging operation sparked additional activity in the area. Their tramway was extended eastward as the timber cutting moved up Washington Gulch. The line ran between Washington Creek and what is now Graham Road. It then divided, with one branch heading northeast along Graham Road and the other bearing southeast along what is now Lindholm Lane (Scha-

Figure 37: Bayside Cutoff area, 1948, showing historical features (HSU Library).

fran 1984; Carranco and Sorensen 1988:212). In May 1876 Dolbeer & Carson had 40 men at work in Washington Gulch. Nearby was a schoolhouse and a blacksmith shop, and several residences were going up. The Henry brothers had just completed a hotel where the tramway crossed the Eureka-Arcata road. The *West Coast Signal* ineffectually suggested "to the people of Jacoby Creek the propriety of adopting the name of 'Carson' for their prosperous little hamlet" (West Coast Signal, May 10, 1876; Schafran 1984).

In 1882 Dolbeer & Carson built a shingle and stave mill west of the Eureka-Arcata road and next to their tramway line (Weekly Humboldt Times, January 7, 1882; Schafran 1984). Eventually Dolbeer & Carson also had a cook house, workers' housing, and railway buildings in the vicinity (Hedlund 1978:63). At an unknown date "[a] small locomotive was later brought in to help bring the logs to tidewater"(Carranco and Sorensen 1988:94). This probably occurred when the wharf was built into Arcata Bay, where, gravitational forces having subsided, additional motive power was needed to move the cars along the nearly level wharf.

Shuster aerial photos of this area show the slough remnant just east of the Redwood Highway. The small structure behind the barn that lies next to Bayside Cutoff was the "main part of the [Carson] shingle mill" (Fountain 2001:(50)171) that once operated next to the tramway. In 1884 logging resumed at Rocky Gulch, with the logs going to the "dumping place at Brainard's Point" (Humboldt Standard, May 5, 1884).

Just south of the Dolbeer and Carson log dump a garbage dump was deployed. In March 1901, after years of unauthorized dumping near the western end of Murray Street (now Del Norte Street),

Figure 38: Brainard Channel, foreground, with pilings from the uncompleted Eureka & Klamath raid line (Humboldt County Public Works).

the Eureka City Council adopted an ordinance establishing a city dump site, this being "a 100 ft. x 166 ft. site on the south side of Murray Street at the southern end of Railroad Avenue and east of the railroad tracks, an area presently part of the PALCO Marsh." In 1925, William S. Clark, owner of the Railroad Avenue property north of the official dump, sued the city because it "had operated a dump not only at the specified site, but . . . it had also 'used and maintained' as a dumping ground Railroad Avenue." The suit prompted the city to pass a garbage ordinance in 1926 that provided "for letting the garbage collection and disposal contract to an individual or firm," along with setting a per-can collection fee and the selection of a new disposal site. Then "the dumps on Railroad Avenue, along nearby streets, and on adjacent lands were officially closed with the enactment of the 1926 ordinance" (Roscoe 1997:4-6).

A replacement dump was apparently established that same year. In August 1926 the Bayside Civic Club took "action to have the garbage dump removed from the Eureka-Arcata state highway marsh," which was otherwise identified as the "A. Batini marsh." The so-called marsh was actu-ally the embattled Brainard Slough. The state highway commission had granted permission for the dump, but the Civic Club members contacted the commission to complain "that the garbage trucks in turning on the road near the dump sometimes held up traffic (Humboldt Times, August 13, 1926). Elsewhere the facility is referred to as the "Batini Dump, a refuse dump that dates to

Figure 39: Brainard Slough area, showing proximity of Batini dump (Humboldt County Public Works).

Figure 40: The mouth of Brainard Slough appears as disregarded as the NWP tracks that hang above it (Aldaron Laird).

the 1930s" (State of California, Office of Historic Preservation 2006). The Batini Dump probably closed in 1933, the year that the Cummings Road Landfill opened as a replacement dump (Call 2020).

Properties belonging to A. Batini and to J. & C. Batini were mapped in 1949 as being directly south of the Dolbeer & Carson log dump area (Metsker 1949:33). Al Batini was co-proprietor of the Ritz Club in Eureka in the 1930s and 1940s (Humboldt Times, April 25, 1934; Humboldt Times, July 18, 1942).

6. Gannon Slough

Gannon Slough, in earlier times called Big Slough or Embarcadero Slough, served as the first supply route between ships on Arcata Bay and Union (Arcata). The slough once "received water from numerous creeks and rivulets off the hillside, and, when it reached the flats, through other sloughs" (Van Kirk 2015:2). In the early days of Union, Gannon Slough provided a less than ideal but workable route for bringing supplies to town: "only small boats could get up the slough. Almost every business firm in Union had a warehouse on Big Slough. These building were built from the main landing on Front Street to the upper landing near Fifth and A streets" (Carranco and Sorensen 1988:3). According to Arcata historian Susie Van Kirk, the lower landing, on Front Street, was on the bay. The upper landing was "somewhere near the present soccer fields and community center" (Van Kirk 2015:4).

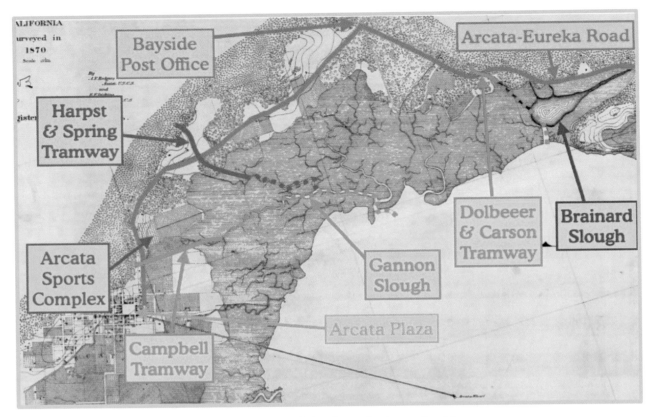

Figure 41: Tramways and sloughs in the Arcata-Bayside area.

The Union Plank Wharf opened in 1855 and supplanted Gannon Slough as Union's main port facility. However, when James Gannon, for whom the slough was eventually named, began logging on upper Campbell Creek (in today's Community Forest) in the 1870s, he used the Campbell tramway to move his logs down to the slough (Van Kirk 2015:4-5).

A second tramway fed into Gannon Slough. John Harpst and O. H. Spring operated a shingle mill at the later-day site of Sunny Brae (Irvine 1915:549-55). Their shingles

> . . . were loaded onto a large wooden car, which had four wheels. This was not a railroad car, although the wheels had flanges on them and were propelled along a crude track made of stringers, with scrap iron nailed on to them. When the shingles were loaded, a mule was loaded on behind and the car proceeded to propel itself down the track . . . . When the car was empty the mule was unloaded, hitched onto the car and made to pull it back to the mill, where the cycle was started all over again (Arcata Union, November 18, 1960).

In 1882 Flanigan, Brosnan and Company built a rail line into the Jacoby Creek drainage to reach their timberlands. The logs they cut there were transported on their railroad to lower Gannon Slough, where a log dump was created. The logs thus dumped floated down the slough to Arcata Bay, where they were made up into rafts that were towed to the company's mill on the west side of Eureka. The rail line was later extended on a wharf out into the bay, whence the logs were then dumped for rafting (Schafran 1984:16-17).

B. Precursor Alternative to a Land Route: Using the Bay

1. Fairhaven Ferry and Mad River Road

Before any road was built between Eureka and Arcata, there was a transportation corridor that allowed wheeled vehicles to make the trip, but it was both inconvenient and unconventional. In September 1854, A. G. Hammon, R. Marvel & Co. announced

> . . . their intention to apply to the Court of Humboldt County for a License to keep a FERRY between Bucksport and West Humboldt [Fairhaven], between the points at which they are now running their Ferry boat (Humboldt Times, September 16, 1854:3).

The ferry's importance was described in an early newspaper article that was grandly (and over-exuberantly) titled,

> Carriage Road to Bucksport
>
> Sheriff Read and Lieutenant Bates came up from Bucksport on Thursday, in a buggy. They crossed in the ferry, at Bucksport, to the North Beach, and followed up the beach to the mouth of Mad River, and reached town by Craig and Denny's new road from that point. This is the first carriage road through and they reported a pleasant trip and a good road (Fountain 1967:(96)38).

Figure 42: Harpst & Spring Shingle Mill at the future site of Sunny Brae (HSU Library).

The ferry route was still functioning in November 1857, when George M. Fay of Bucksport announced that

> The subscriber has established a ferry from Bucksport to the Peninsula and is always in readiness to cross passengers and animals without delay, in good commodious boats. Terms of Ferriage: passengers 50¢ animals $1 (Fountain 1967:(24)254).

It is unclear when travelers between Eureka and Arcata stopped using the ferry and beach route.

2. Ferries across Arcata Bay

By early 1855 the Union [Arcata] Wharf & Plank Walk Company had built both its wharf and, on top of it, a railroad. The wharf ran two miles southward from the Arcata shoreline to a deep water channel in Arcata Bay (Borden 1954a:3-4). The wharf enabled direct ship traffic across the bay between Eureka and Union's new wharf. That January the steamship *Glide* announced runs between Union, Bucksport, and "Jones' Embarcadero" which was located on Salmon Creek in the southeastern corner of the bay (Humboldt Times, January 27, 1855), while the following month Adams & Co. advertised that "the fast sailing clipper yacht *Coquasky* will leave Union daily for Eureka and Bucksport" (Humboldt Times, February 3, 1855).

Figure 43: The ferry *Antelope* at play on Humboldt Bay (HSU Library).

In October 1862 "the staunch little steamer *Laura Ellen*" was "plying the waters of Humboldt Bay" between Eureka and Arcata (Humboldt Times, October 18, 1862.) Over time, several ships regularly made the run. Starting in 1888, the *Antelope*, a paddlewheel steamer operated by the Arcata and Mad River Railroad, ran the route, continuing until 1909 (Redwood Log, July 1953). The steamer *Alta* also followed the channel between Eureka and Arcata, sometimes getting "stuck on the middle ground when the tide was low" (Humboldt Times, January 4, 1931).

C. Railroads

1. The Humboldt Logging Railroad Company

In 1875 the South Bay Railroad Company was created in order to bring logs and lumber from the Salmon Creek area, south of today's College of the Redwoods, to Humboldt Bay. That year it laid six miles of track from Salmon Creek to Fields Landing. The railroad hauled logs for D. R. Jones & Company and lumber from Dolbeer and Carson's Milford Land and Lumber Company until 1880, when the former had cut all its timber in the drainage. Then the railroad—lock, stock, and 34,500-pound Baldwin engine—was moved to Freshwater Creek, where D. R. Jones & Company had started a new logging operation. The rail line became the Humboldt Logging Railroad Company (HLRR). Work started on the new line in early May (Daily Humboldt Times, May 2, 1880), and by August 1 the *Times* could report that "it is certainly a goodly sight to witness a train of cars, loaded with redwood logs and drawn by a locomotive at a good rate of speed, puffing through the valley and across the marsh to tide water" (Daily Humboldt Times, August 1, 1880). By 1881 the HLRR ran along seven miles of track

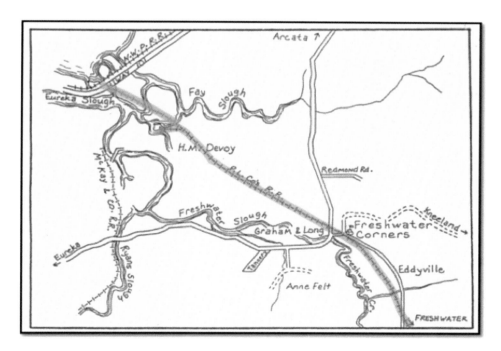

Figure 44: Northern end of HLRR shown in pink. Later Pacific Lumber Company Railroad extension shown in green (Cole 1984).

(Carranco and Sorensen 1988:121-122, 200). In April 1882 the *Times* assessed the rail line's place in the development of the county's log transportation system, indicating that the HLRR

> . . . is the principal enterprise of the kind in the county, and has done much in the past two years toward solving the problem of how to supply the growing demand for redwood lumber. The old method of "running" logs [down a river] has of necessity given place to the steam car, and the great bulk of the timber now standing will in all probability find its way to the mills and to market by this means. Mill men generally recognize this fact, and are providing for the future by building railroads, either for steam or horse-power . . . (Weekly Humboldt Times, April 22, 1882).

In 1886 the line was mapped as extending from near the confluence of Freshwater and Fay Sloughs up the Freshwater Valley to the town of Freshwater, with spur lines running east up Mc-Cready, Cloney, and Graham gulches (Forbes 1886).

2. The Eureka & Freshwater Railroad

A new timber enterprise, the California Redwood Company (CRC), was formed in 1883. It purchased the holdings of three other lumber firms, including that of D. R. Jones & Company. As part of the transaction, the CRC took over operation of the Humboldt Logging Railroad Company, although it did not change its name. The CRC became involved in a massive timberland fraud scheme and suspended operations in 1885. The following year the Excelsior Redwood Company was formed in order to salvage vestiges of the CRC (Carranco and Sorensen 1988:122-123). One

Figure 45: Excelsior Redwood Company trains near Freshwater Corners, c. 1891, showing three trains of logs and one (far right) with rock for the Humboldt Bay jetties (Jack Irvine Collection).

Figure 46: Yellow arrow points to remnant of Freshwater Landing, south of Murray Field; cerise arrow points to Pacific Lumber Company Railroad grade (Humboldt County Public Works).

vestige was the HLRR, which again retained its name (Hamm 1890:67). It reportedly took "the first rock for Humboldt Bay's jetties," which was hauled from Graham and McCready gulches, far up the Freshwater Valley (Van Kirk 2006c:31).

Excelsior logged in the Freshwater area until 1893, by which time it had leveled all its timberland there (Carranco and Sorensen 1988:123). After six years "of almost solemn quiet," in 1899 the woodman's ax once more was heard in the forests of Freshwater, and the "iron pathways" of the HLRR were again readied for service (Blue Lake Advocate, June 24, 1899). Then, in September 1900, the owners of the Excelsior Redwood Company incorporated the Eureka & Freshwater Railway Company (E&F), claiming it would build 12 miles of track, although the incorporators already owned the HLRR, which had almost that much trackage already in place. The real news was the location where the E&F would have to add track—between the landing on Freshwater Slough and Eureka. At last it appeared that trains from the Freshwater Valley would run all the way to the city (Arcata Union, September 1, 1900).

But not entirely over their own tracks. In August 1901 the E&F signed an agreement with the California & Northern Railway (C&N), which had a right-of-way along the bay shore, whereby the E&F would connect its tracks, which would come north from Freshwater Landing, with the C&N's at a location later named Freshwater Junction. From there the E&F trains would travel on the C&N's tracks to Eureka and back (Borden 1963a:10).

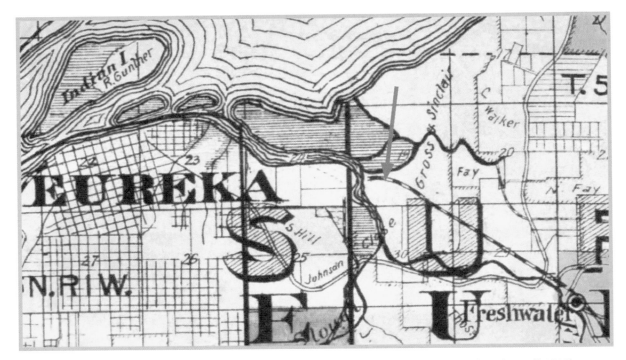

Figure 47: An 1898 map showing the E&F's rail line ending at Freshwater Landing (Lentell 1898).

In April 1903 associates of the Pacific Lumber Company formed the Freshwater Lumber Company, which then purchased the Excelsior Lumber Company's timberlands in the Freshwater area and Excelsior's E&F rail line (Borden 1949:10). By September workers were clearing "out the old railroad which was abandoned years ago by the Excelsior Company" (Daily Humboldt Times, September 3, 1903).

The E&F at the time owned 14 miles of track, four locomotives, and numerous logging cars. Plans were made "to build a large mill and town to be known as Eddyville in the area" (Carranco and Sorensen 1988:138), with the lumber being shipped out on the E&F. In August 1904 work had started on Eddyville, which was located about a half-mile southeast of Freshwater Corners, when a lawsuit enjoined the E&F from connecting with the San Francisco & Northwestern, the current name of the bayshore rail line (Borden 1949a:10).

The Pacific Lumber Company (PL) controlled the Freshwater Lumber Company, and through it, the E&F. PL was embroiled in a complicated corporate chess game to see which local lumber companies would gain railroad access to the San Francisco Bay Area, a contretemps that threatened to expand into a bruising battle for coveted rights-of-way and that had come to involve forces of power far greater than those found in Humboldt County, namely the Santa Fe and Southern Pacific railroads (Rohde 2014b:30-33).

Unable to gain an outlet for the E&F, PL moved its "machinery, supplies and equipment" from Eddyville-to-be to the company's homeland at Scotia (Borden 1949a:10) as its new president, Selwyn Eddy, looked wistfully at the blank space on the map where the name "Eddyville" had been slated to appear (Rohde 2014b:33).

3. The Pacific Lumber Company Railroad

Another reorganization of the Pacific Lumber Company occurred in 1905, with PL absorbing the Freshwater Lumber Company. By 1906 PL was logging its recently acquired timberlands in the Freshwater area. That year the company, no longer under court injunction, extended the tracks of what was now called the Pacific Lumber Company Railroad one and one-half miles northward, bypassing its log dump and wharf at Freshwater Landing. PL thus finally made the long-awaited connection with the bayside rail line, which was now owned by a new but short-lived enterprise called the San Francisco & Northwestern Railway, which, in January 1907, became the Northwestern Pacific Railroad (NWP). The logs being taken from Freshwater went not to PL's Scotia mill, however, but instead went to the Holmes Eureka Lumber Company's mill at Bucksport. Selling logs to a rival timber company proved to be an audacious but brief escapade. Later in 1907 PL concluded its Freshwater logging foray and moved its remaining equipment to Scotia (Carranco and Sorensen 1988:53, 141).

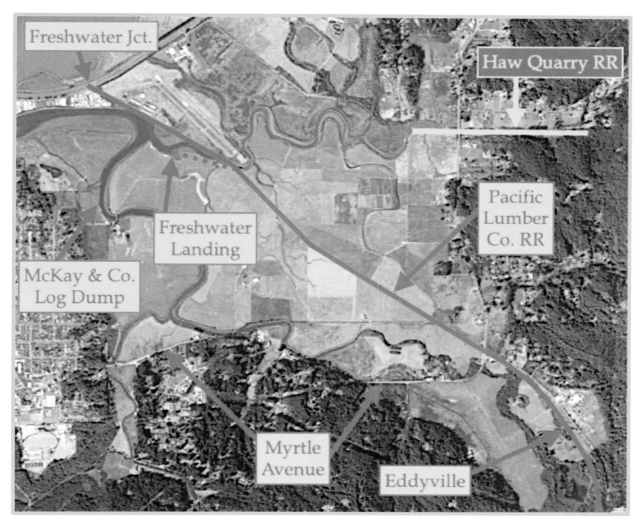

Figure 48: Northern end of the Pacific Lumber Company Railroad and other nearby features (aerial photo from Apple Maps 2020).

Figure 49: While auto traffic waits, a Pacific Lumber Company engine hauls empties crosses Highway 101 in 1940. Steam from the engine is visible to the right of the Murray Field hangar (Humboldt County Public Works).

By 1916 PL was back again in the Freshwater drainage. It resuscitated Eddyville by making it the site of its initial logging camp, an act that came too late to be appreciated by Selwyn Eddy, who had died five years earlier (Carranco and Sorensen 1988:147; Bay Journal 2020a). PL's rail line was subsequently extended ten miles up South Freshwater Creek in an elaborate system that included four inclines. Logs from Freshwater were now taken to Freshwater Junction, where PL's tracks met those of the NWP, and from there traveled south to PL's mill at Scotia.

PL stopped logging at Freshwater in 1924; it resumed cutting there in 1927 but halted again in 1941 (Carranco and Sorensen 1988:147, 149). Meanwhile, Freshwater Junction had become an exciting place, for it was there that the right-of-ways of PL's rail line and the Redwood Highway crossed. Whenever a PL log train came to the junction, highway traffic halted. It was a situation difficult to imagine happening today.

In August 1941 PL removed vestiges of its "old time logging railroad" that had transported the redwood logs of Freshwater for over 60 years (Humboldt Standard, August 17, 1941). The tracks were gone, but the causeway upon which they had rested was still in place, serving as a dikelike barrier that now ran, for the most part without purpose, across the wetlands. At its western end, however, the causeway did serve to buffer the Murray Field airport from the east end of Eureka Slough, a function that it still performs to this day.

Figure 50: No longer needed. Abandoned water tank next to abandoned rails at Eddyville (author's collection).

Figure 51: Pacific Lumber Company Railroad causeway, center, between Murray Field, left, and the Farm Store, right (Jerry Rohde).

4. The Flanigan, Brosnan & Company Railroad

In 1876 four partners—D.J. Flanigan, Timothy Brosnan, John Harpst, and James Gannon—started a lumber business called Flanigan, Brosnan, and Company (FB&C). They built a mill at the foot of Whipple (now 14th) Street in Eureka and acquired some redwood acreage in the Jacoby Creek drainage. The company also put in a standard gauge rail line that ran up the north side of the Jacoby Creek valley (Carranco and Sorensen 1988:86); it began operating in 1882 (Schafran 1984:16).

The FB&C put up several buildings in what became Bayside, including a shingle mill, cookhouse, store, four-stall train engine house, warehouse, and several cabins for their workers (Carranco and Sorensen 1988:86). These were located southwest of the corner that the Eureka-Arcata road formed just south of the current Bayside post office. The rail line came down the canyon on the southern side of today's Jacoby Creek Road, passing between the Grange Hall and the Good Templars' Hall (Schafran 1984). It then ran northwest for about a mile before bending west. At first the tracks ended at Gannon Slough, where the FB&C built a log dump. This allowed their logs to be

Figure 52: FB&C log dump on Gannon Slough (HSU Library).

rolled into the slough, from where they would be floated to the bay, made into log rafts, and taken to the FB&C's Bayside Mill in Eureka (Schafran 1984:16-17).

In 1900 a new business, the Bayside Mill and Lumber Company, acquired Flanigan, Brosnan and Company. Five years later this second company was purchased by Levi Smith, who was affiliated with the Warren Timber Company of Pennsylvania (Roberts 1972:4). The new enterprise dropped the "mill" from the earlier name, becoming the Bayside Lumber Company (BLC), a timely decision since the mill burned shortly thereafter. The structure was soon rebuilt, however, and it cut logs from not just Jacoby Creek but also from newly acquired BLC forestland on the Van Duzen River and at Nanning Creek.

The rail line carried more than logs and shingles. In 1891 the FB&C agreed to supply Simpson & Brown, who were constructing the Humboldt Bay jetties, with "50,000 ton of rock and haul it to deep water." The rock would come from the FB&C's quarries on upper Jacoby Creek. To reach "deep water," the company extended its rail line from Gannon Slough westward, building a wharf to take the tracks out into the bay (Arcata Union, January 31, 1891).

The wharf eventually extended a mile and a half into the bay. Near its western end it bent southwest to avoid bumping into the preexisting Arcata Wharf (Schafran 1984:16-17). The wharf ended at a channel in Arcata Bay that was, at that point, six feet deep (Coast Survey 1916). This allowed ships of appropriate draft to load two cargoes from the wharf, quarried rock and shingles. An undated photo of the wharf shows it stacked with shingles, with several sailing ships tied up ready to load

Figure 53: The bounty of Bayside: logs (left) and shingles (right), probably at Gannon Slough, c. 1910 (HSU Library).

them. A short distance to the south, a tugboat tows a raft filled with small railcars that are carrying quarry rock for the South Jetty.

The wharf was built under the supervision of D. J. Flanigan and was reputedly "the most substantial piece of work in the county over tide water. The big locomotive and tender, weighing 45 tons, does not shake it" (Arcata Union, September 5, 1891). So sturdy was the wharf that a row of its piling still anchors the edge of Arcata Marsh's easternmost oxidation pond.

Sturdiness was needed not just for the locomotive but also for the loads of jetty rock that it sometimes hauled to the bay. The Arcata Union described the transfer of rock-carrying rail cars at the FB&C wharf. The FB&C engine brought down 21 cars, each filled with 10 tons or more of rock. A "railroad scow" that had three sets of tracks running along its deck transported the rock. It came up to a loading "apron" that was attached to the wharf. The FB&C locomotive then moved seven of the rock cars onto each of the three sets of tracks (Arcata Union, September 5, 1891). Thus the wharf supported not just the 45-ton engine but 21 rock cars carrying a total of at least 210 tons of rock.

Figure 54: Flanigan, Brosnan and Company's Shingle Wharf, looking east. Shingles line the wharf, while rock from the company's quarry is being towed by the tugboat (HSU Library).

Figure 55: Flanigan, Brosnan and Company's wharf piling adjacent the oxidation pond (Jerry Rohde).

Sturdy the wharf was, but this was little protection against events on the evening of May 30, 1900. At about 6:00 P.M., with some 4,000,000 shingles stacked in piles five feet high on the wharf, ready for shipment, the FB&C's locomotive emitted a spark while steaming along the structure. It landed "directly in the center of the shingle wharf," starting a small fire that quickly spread to the partly dried shingles. Word of the impending disaster soon reached Bayside, and the FB&C's shingle mill workers rushed down to help the embattled train crew in trying extinguish the blaze. With no fire-fighting equipment on hand, some of the workers formed a bucket brigade while others removed shingles that were in the fire's path. For a time it looked as if all would be lost, but then new forces intervened.

The first intervention came from gravity, which exerted its indomitable power upon a fire-weakened section of the wharf, causing it to collapse. Gone in a trice were some 2,000,000 shingles, many of which the fire had ruined anyway, and gone also was a substantial section of the wharf, thereby creating a sort of aqueous firebreak that slowed the flames' spread.

Meanwhile, the illumination caused by the conflagration was such that by 7:00 P.M. its glow was noticed across the bay in Eureka. Residents of the city stared northward at the spectacle, but more than an hour elapsed before FB&C co-owner Timothy Brosnan learned of the fire and took action. Now events moved quickly:

Fugure 56: Twenty-one carloads of Jacoby Creek Quarry rock arrive at the unloading apron on the South Spit
(HSU Library).

The shrieking of the Antelope's whistle about 8:30 o'clock called her captain and crew together. Many of
the townspeople also heard the unusual noise and rushed to the steamer's dock. Among these were many
members of the Eureka Fire Department, and when informed as to the situation they immediately tendered
their assistance. This was gladly accepted, and after the Antelope had been made ready and a quantity of
fire apparatus secured from the engine house, she proceeded with all possible speed for the Bayside [wharf]
apron. The relief crew arrived shortly after 9:00 o'clock. No time was lost and in a few minutes two streams
of water were playing on the burning wharf and the floating mass of shingles (Humboldt Times, May 31,
1900).

Now a new danger presented itself. The tide was rising, and it moved the floating, but still flam-
ing, shingles and debris under unburnt sections of the wharf, threatening to ignite new fires on the
underside of the planking. It was a novel situation for the experienced fire fighters from Eureka, but
they were up to the task and, helped by the arrival of the bar tug Ranger at about 10 P.M., the flames
were subdued (Humboldt Times, May 31, 1900).

In the aftermath, Brosnan found that although the fire was spectacular, it was not as destructive
as first thought. The planking from part of the wharf was lost, but the piling that supported it was
still in good condition. Of the 2,000,000 shingles that dropped into the bay, only about half were

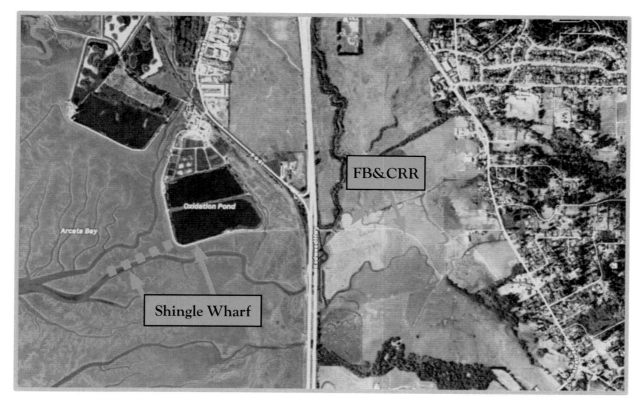

Figure 57: Route of FB&C rail line northwest of Bayside (aerial photo from Apple Maps 2020).

ruined. A boom of logs was put around the soggy but salvageable shingles to keep them from floating away on the tide. The loss was only about $2,000, and "the tired and watersoaked firemen" had a story worth telling for years to come (Humboldt Times, May 31, 1900).

By December 1913 the Jacoby Creek timberlands had been logged out. It was reported that "Newell's Camp here has shut down for good. Bayside Mill and Lumber Co. has cut here for 30 years and will now get its log supply from southern Humboldt" (Fountain 2001:(50)290). The rail line, however, was still used to transport rock from the quarries, not always a safe activity. In April 1915 there was an accident near the upper quarry when a "gasoline track car" jumped the tracks and all four riders were thrown into the Jacoby Creek gulch, killing Morton L. Tower (Arcata Union, April 22, 1915). And in April 1920 a logging train had two cars leave the tracks at the lower quarry (Arcata Union, March 18, 1920). It is unclear exactly when the railroad ceased operating, but a 1923 newspaper article indicated that "the rails on the old Bayside railroad were taken up some time ago . . ." (Blue Lake Advocate, July 28, 1923).

5. The McKay & Company Railroad

Having sent their logs careening down Ryan Slough on the seasonal freshets since 1875, McKay & Co. developed a more sophisticated transport system in 1883. That June it was reported that they

. . . had determined to build a railroad from tide water along Ryan's Slough to a point opening up their timber and furnishing them with certain means of transportation of timber to the mill. This slough has always seen drives, but of late years many obstacles were encountered. . . .

The present [railroad] grade is two miles long, extending from the county bridge [just downslough from today's Myrtle Avenue] to the dam, just above the old Connick camp" (Daily Times-Telephone, June 21, 1883).

Initially the rail line ran from just south of Myrtle Avenue up the Ryan Creek canyon to a point roughly due east of the current Humboldt Bay Community Services District plant on Walnut Drive (Forbes 1886). At the terminus near Myrtle Avenue was a landing where McKay & Co. dumped their logs into Ryan Slough, whence they were floated down Ryan, Freshwater, and Eureka sloughs to the bay and then towed to the company's Occidental Mill at the northwest edge of Eureka. In 1887 the company extended their rail line about three-quarters mile northward to a point just north of what is now the eastern end of Myrtletown's Park Street. Here they built a new landing that allowed them

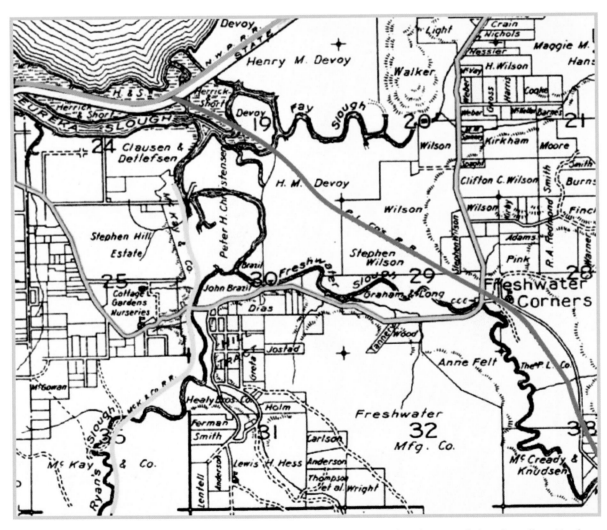

Figure 58: In 1922 the McKay and Co. railroad (orange) ran north to their log dump and shingle mill on Freshwater Slough. The Pacific Lumber Company Railroad (purple) went north to Freshwater Junction, where it connected with the Northwestern Pacific Railroad (pink). The Eureka-Arcata road (green) crossed the wetlands west of Freshwater Corners (Belcher Abstract & Title Co.)

Figure 59: McKay & Co. shingle mill, Freshwater Slough (HSU Library).

to dump their logs into the larger Freshwater Slough (California State Supreme Court 1906:100). At the new northern terminus of the rail line, McKay & Co. also constructed a small train yard, with repair shops and an engine house (Carranco and Sorensen 1988:82). With the new terminus came trouble. It arrived as follows: south of Myrtle Avenue, the McKay & Co. tracks passed through the property of Charles W. Hill. A dispute arose in 1888 regarding a part of the right-of-way agreement. The case was litigated all the way to the California Supreme Court, which ruled that damages assessed by the lower courts against McKay & Co. were excessive, and granted a new trial (California State Supreme Court 1906:21).

It was a Pyrrhic victory for McKay & Co. They might have won the court case, but they had long ago lost the goodwill of Hill, who in 1891 revoked the right-of-way agreement for the rail line (Genzoli 1973:54). This meant that more than a half-mile of track through Hill's property south of Myrtle Avenue had to be rerouted westward onto McKay land. The result was the county's only railroad "shunnel," a hybrid structure that appeared to be part tunnel and part shed roof. It was actually a cut in the hillside that ran just inside the McKay & Co. property line. However, "because of the narrow space between the track and the Hill property it was necessary to board the cut on both sides and roof it over to keep Hill's property from caving in and sliding onto the track" (Carranco and

Figure 60: McKay & Co. log dump on Freshwater Slough, north of Park Street (Aldaron Laird).

Sorensen 1988:83-84). The "shunnel" cut through the hillside within today's McKay Community Forest about a quarter-mile east of Redwood Acres.

In 1890 what was referred to as the "Ryans' [sic] Slough Railroad" was now "about six miles in length, from tide-water to a magnificent belt of redwood, and the valley through which it passes is very fertile" (Hamm 1890:69) The 1898 county map shows the railroad still at this approximate length, having penetrated the Ryan Creek drainage to a point about a mile east-northeast of today's Ridgewood Heights (Lentell 1898).

By 1911 the rail line had extended to its farthest southern limit, running up the west fork of Ryan Creek to a location about one mile south of Ridgewood Heights (Denny 1911). Sometime between 1911 and 1921 a branch line was run from Ryan Creek eastward up Bear Gulch (Belcher Abstract & Title Co. 1921:6).

The railroad, and the loggers, kept busy. A June 1900 report stated:

> The times are lively these days up Ryan's Slough. There are 85 men employed with 11 sets of choppers at work. The daily output is about 100,000 feet of logs and about six trainloads of logs are dumped at the mouth of the slough each day. At present there is in the slough between 2 and 3 million [board] feet of logs and it is expected to put in about 23 million more this season (Genzoli 1973:33).

In 1902 McKay & Co. built a shingle mill at the rail line's northern terminus (Genzoli 1973:34). They upgraded this operation in September 1907 with a "huge Sturtevant hot air blower" that could "dry 200,000 shingles every twenty-four hours." The mill itself had been "recently rebuilt over the ashes of a comparatively new mill," which did not have a drying plant (San Francisco Chronicle 1903a:7). The shingle mill was located immediately west of Freshwater Slough about 300 yards northwest of the end of Park Avenue (Belcher and Crane Company 1916).

The rail line that ran up the Ryan Creek canyon stayed close to the creek in order to maintain a moderate grade. It crossed the stream several times and in places ran above the top of the creek itself on sections of trestle (Belcher Abstract and Title Co. 1921:6, 7). One trestle piling remains; it juts from the creek in the stark solitude of a forgotten remnant (Rohde 2014a). Frank Cerny, a long-time resident of the area, recalled seeing a trestle near the confluence of Ryan Creek and Henderson Gulch that "ran south for about 200 yards." Cerny indicated "that most of the railroad grade was on solid ground, with only portions of it on elevated trestles." A spur line up Bear Gulch "ran right up the creek channel" (Cerny 2007). The northern section of the line was built mostly on fill to carry it above the wetlands of Ryan Slough. Part of PG&E's gas line now follows the elevated grade, both upstream and downstream from the Myrtle Avenue bridge. The northernmost section of the rail line is visible from Park Street as a blackberry-covered causeway that separates dairy land to the east from a wetland to the west (Rohde 2014a).

Figure 61: McKay & Co. #1 near the Freshwater Slough log dump (Humboldt County Historical Society).

The Occidental Mill continued operations into the 1930s, when it fell victim to the Great Depression. It closed in 1930, but reopened briefly in 1931 and 1932 (Carranco and Sorensen 1988:84-85). The possibility for further activity ended on September 12, 1934, when the mill "was totally . . . destroyed by one of the most spectacular fires in Humboldt history." The noontime conflagration "threw showers of burning cinders over a large part of the city and repeatedly threatened to spread into the business district." In desperation, the Eureka fire department called on the harbor steamer *Antelope*, the Coast Guard cutter *Cahokia*, the tug *Humboldt*, and the fire car of the Northwestern Pacific Railroad to help quench the flames (Humboldt Times, September 13, 1934). No Viking funeral could have exceeded the dramatic departure of the oldest mill in Eureka.

And that was it for the logging operations of McKay & Co. The mill was never rebuilt. Most of the Ryan Creek old-growth forest that fed it was gone, and it would be more than a decade before another timber boom had lumbermen looking longingly at the tract's trees. Both McKay locomotives were scrapped in 1935, most of their remains reposing at Breeden's bayside junk yard. The boiler of the McKay engine #2, the J. J. Loggie, endured, however. It was first moved to Hayfork, in Trinity County, where it powered a small sawmill until 1947. Subsequently it was taken by Henry Sorensen to his railroad museum in McKinleyville (Carranco and Sorensen 1988:84-85), making it most of the way back to the McKay Tract.

As for the tract's tracks, they were removed, probably for a World War II scrap drive. Richard Philipsen, who explored the area in the 1950s with his boyhood friend, Roger Rodoni, recalled that by then no rails remained along the railroad grade, only ties (Philipsen 2014a).

Figure 62; The Occidental Mill used part of Humboldt Bay for its log pond (thehumboldtproject.org).

Figure 63: The McKay & Co. railbed, left, isolated a small section of wetland, right (Aldaron Laird)

A lasting effect of the rail line's extension to the McKay shingle mill was the cordoning off of a section of wetland between Myrtle Avenue and Park Street. As usual, the causeway upon which the railroad was built served as a dike, separating the wetlands to the east from a wetland fragment between the railroad grade and the hillslope at the eastern edge of Myrtletown. About one thousand feet north of Myrtle Avenue, McKay & Co. installed a culvert at the base of the railroad grade to allow the wetland fragment to drain into Ryan Slough, but over time the culvert ceased to be maintained and water was no longer able flow through it. In 2003 a nearby resident contacted the property's owner, which at the time was Simpson Timber Company, to complain that water had risen in the wetland fragment to the point where it was encroaching on his property. Simpson had not been aware of the culvert prior to this; they then had a new part fashioned for the culvert and installed it, which allowed the historic but still important feature to resume its function of providing drainage (Templeton 2020).

6. The Haw Quarry Railroad

A rock quarry was located in the northeast quarter of the southeast quarter of Section 21, Township 5 North, Range 1 East, Humboldt Meridian, at the eastern end of today's Quail Valley Road. It was sold in 1880 by William Carson to brothers Nahum and George M. Fay. It is not known if

Figure 64: Haw Quarry Railroad trestle and wharf visible at head of Fay Slough during a 1948 flood (HSU Library).

Carson quarried there, but the Fay brothers did. An ambiguous report suggests they were running it in the spring of 1889 and that in 1890 they were using the quarry to supply rock to the jetties at the mouth of Humboldt Bay (Van Kirk 2007a:16). A January 1896 article in the *Humboldt Standard* considered possible sources of rock to macadamize the City of Eureka's streets. The writer indicated that "the finest rock yet seen by the author is a sample from the Fay Brother's quarry near Freshwater" (Daily Humboldt Standard, January 25, 1896).

Apparently prompted by the newspaper report, two weeks later the city entered into a contract that allowed the Fays to operate the quarry and extract from it rock at the rate "of four cents per ton, payable yearly in gold coin" (Humboldt County Deeds 57:319). The city apparently transported the rock along what is now known as Quail Valley Road (Van Kirk 2007a:17).

Early in 1908 W. H. Haw contracted to supply crushed rock from the quarry to the City of Eureka (Van Kirk 2007a:18). Haw hired Fred Houda to supervise construction of a one-mile railroad (Daily Humboldt Times, March 29, 1908) that ran along the valley north of Quail Valley Road and ended at a wharf at the upper end of Fay Slough (Van Kirk 2007a:18). The rock was transported from the hillside quarry to the valley floor on a railed incline; a steam donkey at the quarry lowered and raised the railcars (Van Kirk 2006a:13). The cars were then moved onto the mile-long Haw Quarry Railroad where they were pulled to the wharf by a Marshutz & Cantrell locomotive to the Fay Slough wharf. There the railcars were loaded onto barges and first taken down Fay Slough and then Eureka Slough to Humboldt Bay and thence to Eureka (Van Kirk 207a:18; Daily Humboldt Times, July 11, 1908).

Haw's railroad was finished in June (Daily Humboldt Times, June 7, 1908) but his transport system soon encountered difficulties. In August, the conveyor system at the City's gravel bunkers, which were located at the foot of J Street, was tested but failed to operate properly (Daily Humboldt Times, August 18, 1908). The problem was soon remedied, but then, in early September,

> one of the heavily laden rock rafts of Contractor W. H. Haw, who is getting crushed rock out of the quarry at Freshwater for the City of Eureka, while being towed down the slough at Freshwater last Tuesday night, stuck the drawbridge of the Freshwater railroad company, owned by the Pacific Lumber Company, putting it out of commission for several days.
>
> The heavy, unwieldy craft was coming down the waterway in tow of a launch at a pretty fast rate, and just before the bridge was reached, it swung to one side, striking the piling and throwing the bridge several inches out of plumb.
>
> The trains of the lumber company, which were hauling bolts, were hung up for several days until a crew of carpenters were able to repair the damage, and to guard against further accidents of the same kind, a pile driver crew was put to work constructing sheer booms to ward [off] the passing rafts from the bridge piling.
>
> Fearful lest they should be treated the same way, the Freshwater Investment Co. had one of the Mercer-Fraser pile drivers drive piling to construct a similar sheer boom to protect their drawbridges, which is [sic] located on the same slough. Both jobs are now completed and there is no danger that the rock rafts will do any damage to the bridges (Daily Humboldt Standard, September 12, 1908).

The California State Mining Bureau reported on the quarry in 1915, at which time it was owned by G. A. Dungan and I. M. Long. It consisted of 700 acres of mountainside at an elevation of 150 feet. The rock being quarried was "a basaltic lava termed tachylyte." It had a specific gravity of 3,169 and was 42.7 per cent silica. The "standard gauge" railroad was still one mile long (Lowell 1915:22), allowing it to remain the shortest short line in Humboldt County (Rohde forthcoming). In addition to the Haw locomotive the transportation equipment consisted of "eleven bottom dump cars, one barge, [and] one tow boat." Various mining equipment was present, as were "a cookhouse, blacksmith shop, powder house, and several smaller buildings" (Lowell 1915:22).

In 1916 Eureka voters authorized the purchase of Haw's quarry equipment and the rights to remove rock from the quarry site (Van Kirk 2017a:18). According to the agreement, the use of the rock had expanded: the city would "pay four cents per ton for all building and curbing stone and six cents per cubic yard for the first 10,000 yards of crushed rock removed during any one year," with a drop in price for additional crushed rock taken during a single year. The agreement was to remain in effect for 40 years (Humboldt Times, November 29, 1916), which indicated that the City lacked foresight in anticipating improvements in accessing street paving materials. *Greatly* lacked foresight, it turned out. By September 1921, less than five years after signing the forty-year agreement, the Eureka City Council found that "private producers" could more cheaply provide rock for the city streets, rendering the quarry "valueless." Mayor A. C. Dauphiny "suggested" that the quarry "be sold to the highest bidder" (Humboldt Standard, September 30, 1921).

Figure 65: Remnants of the Haw Quarry Railroad trestle as seen from Walker Point, c. 2010 (Jerry Rohde).

The quarry probably ceased operating about this time. Nearby resident Sandy Wilson indicated that he was certain the quarry had closed by 1925 if not earlier. In the 1930s Ike Moxon found that the Haw Railroad ties were still in place but the rails had been removed (Van Kirk 2007a:19). Remnants of the trestle over the wetland and to the wharf on Fay Slough were still visible in an aerial photo from 1948 and even today the blackberry covered skeleton of the trestle can be seen west of Myrtle Avenue.

7. The Northwestern Pacific Railroad (NWP)

By the 1880s short lines had been run from Lindsay Creek, Freshwater Slough, Ryan Slough, and Salmon Creek to tidewater. This was fine as far as it went, but mill owners wanted to improve the other end of the transportation system—a trans-county railroad that would allow them to ship Humboldt County lumber to the Bay Area. Other businesses and the general public also liked the idea, since it would reduce reliance on sea travel, which was sometimes dangerous and often undependable.

Thus began the era of mainline railroad competition.

Two forces arrayed themselves in opposition to one another. In November 1882 lumbermen

John Vance and William Carson joined with other local plutocrats to create the Eel River and Eureka Railroad (ER&ERR). A week later the Pacific Lumber Company formed the competing Humboldt Bay and Eel River Railroad (HB&ERRR). Presently the rival companies decided to compromise, with the ER&ERR laying track that by 1885 connected the end points given in its name, while PL built a branch line that ran from its Scotia mill site northward to meet the ER&ERR tracks at Alton (Rohde 2014b:28-30, 337-338). This temporarily settled the issue, but more maneuvering was in store.

Time passed, and the rival lumber interests lumbered into positions designed to provide exclusive control over key sections of railroad rights-of-way, the most crucial of which became the one through the bayside properties between Eureka and Arcata. It was here that rail lines in the northern part of the county came into play.

In 1874 Eureka lumberman John Vance had created the Humboldt and Mad River Railroad to carry lumber from his Big Bonanza Mill at the mouth of Lindsay Creek to Mad River Slough. Three years later the rail line was also carrying his larger logs, which were too big for the Big Bonanza Mill to cut and were instead taken from Mad River Slough by scows to his mill at the foot of G Street in Eureka. Vance died in January 1892 and his G Street mill burned two months later. His nephew, John M. Vance, took charge. A replacement mill was built across the bay at what became Samoa, and in 1896 the company started a new rail line, the Eureka & Klamath River Railroad (E&KRRR). At first it ran from the Samoa mill to Lindsay Creek, south of Fieldbrook, but as its name indicated, it aspired to operating over a greater distance (Carranco and Sorensen 1988:33, 36-37). On March 4, 1899, the E&KRRR was granted a franchise to lay track from Arcata Junction (near today's skateboard park) south along E Street on its way towards Eureka (Borden 1958a:7).

A year and a day later, the California & Northern Railway (C&N) was incorporated. Among its incorporators were Charles Nelson of the Pacific Lumber Company; Francis Korbel of the Northern Redwood Lumber Company; P. L. Flanigan of Flanigan, Brosnan & Co., which operated Eureka's Bayside Mill; and John L. Koster, president of the California Barrel Company (Borden 1963a:9; Carranco 1982:199; National Coopers' Journal 1907a:16). The rail line thus represented the interests of four Humboldt County timber companies. Like the E&KRRR, the C&N's vision was northward; it hoped, in defiance of the manifold geomorphological obstacles placed in its way by the unsympathetic processes of Nature, to connect the northwestern California county seats of Eureka and Crescent City (Carranco and Sorensen 1988:38), and, more importantly, gain rail access to the redwood-rich forests that lay between the two cities.

But first another space between cities had to be considered. Both rail lines needed to connect Eureka with Arcata before serious work could move northward. In the 366 days since gaining its franchise through Arcata, the E&KRRR had built southward down E Street 2.5 miles from Arcata Junction, crossing the Flanigan, Brosnan & Company's tracks near the southern end of Arcata and the Harpst & Spring tramway at Gannon Slough. The C&N cast its appraising eye over these glinting rails and promptly offered to buy out the E&KRRR (Borden 1958a:7).

Figure 66: C&N lift bridge over Eureka Slough (HSU Library).

The E&KRRR, which had also appraised the situation, refused to sell. Soon the C&N challenged the E&KRRR by laying track. As the E&KRRR worked south from Arcata, the C&N constructed a drawbridge over Eureka Slough and built north from there upon the bayside mud flats (Borden 1961a:13).

Then Andrew B. Hammond entered the fray. Already a successful timberman in Montana and Oregon, in early 1900 he formed the Hammond Lumber Company. Five months later the acquisitive Hammond acquired the Vance Lumber Company, including the E&KRRR (Gordon 2014:195, 225; Borden 1958a:80).

Hammond, an outsider just starting to cut the forests of northwestern California, took the long view regarding the relationship between railroads and redwoods. According to Hammond biographer Greg Gordon, "Hammond realized that Humboldt County would be the final railroad frontier in the continental United States. This was where the great railroad powers—the Santa Fe and Southern Pacific—would play out their game for control of California's transcontinental traffic. Gaining access to Humboldt County, the state's largest timber producer, would be a coup for a railroad with imperial ambitions" (Gordon 2014:259). So it was that the contest between Hammond's E&KRRR and the C&N intensified.

Figure 67: This 1947 photo shows the NWP's Warren Truss swing bridge that replaced the original lift bridge in 1916 (HSU Library).

Both lines sought a franchise that would allow them to build through Eureka along the waterfront. On April 8, 1901 the C&N obtained this authorization (Borden 1963a:9). It was possible that the E&KRRR would soon be granted a similar franchise, but there was a section of the city, east of J Street, where the constricted topography permitted only a single set of tracks (Borden 1961a:13). How would the competing companies deal with this difficulty?

The answer came at 12:01 a.m. on Sunday, April 22, when a crew of C&N workers, by stealth of night, began laying track westward from their Eureka Slough bridge. With no court available on the Sabbath at which to seek an injunction, Hammond looked on helplessly as the C&N's rails were extended all the way to J Street, thereby gaining possession of the narrow, single track right-of-way east of there (Borden 1961a:13; Carranco and Sorensen 1988:41).

Here was high drama worthy of a movie treatment, which it in fact received in 1927 in *The Valley of the Giants* (Humboldt Standard, September 11, 1927). The real time action continued as the C&N obtained its franchise from the City of Eureka on April 30 and immediately put down rails from the end of the E&KRRR's trackage at J Street westward to B Street, where the northern terminus of the preexisting Eel River and Eureka Railroad offered a route south (Borden 1961:14). There were now two railroads through north Eureka's waterfront, but they did not connect.

Stalemate.

Then, on July 22, 1901, each company conveyed a half-interest in their Eureka trackage to their competitor so that both lines could run through town. Two weeks later, a third line, the Eureka & Freshwater Railway, realizing that there was no room to run its tracks into Eureka, made an agreement with the C&N to connect the two lines at Freshwater Junction (near later-day Murray Field) and then run their trains on the C&N's tracks through Eureka (Borden 1961:14).

On September 1 the C&N completed its line along Eureka's waterfront. Later that month the C&N bought the offices of the Excelsior Redwood Company at the foot of F Street for use as a passenger station and company offices. On October 9 the C&N and the E&KRRR joined their tracks in Eureka as per their recent agreement. The results were as follows: there was a single line through northeastern Eureka to J Street. At that point the C&N had run its tracks on an arc north of First Street that served the buildings on the waterfront, while the E&KRRR's tracks ran west directly down First Street. Near B Street the lines briefly rejoined before meeting the trackage of Eureka & Eel River near A Street (Borden 1963a:10; Sanborn Map Company 1920).

Meanwhile, rail building activity continued between Eureka and Arcata. The C&N pushed northward along the edge of Arcata Bay until it reached an obstacle known as Brainard's Point, the fishhook-shaped protuberance of ridgeline that started near Indianola and terminated next to the bay at what is now called Bracut. The C&N began cutting through this obstruction by using 48 teams of horses to remove earth from the ridge. When this system proved too slow the horses were replaced, in December 1900, by two steam shovels (Fountain 2001:(50)86). Four months later observers on the Arcata wharf could look eastward to see that "the precipitous sides of the opening

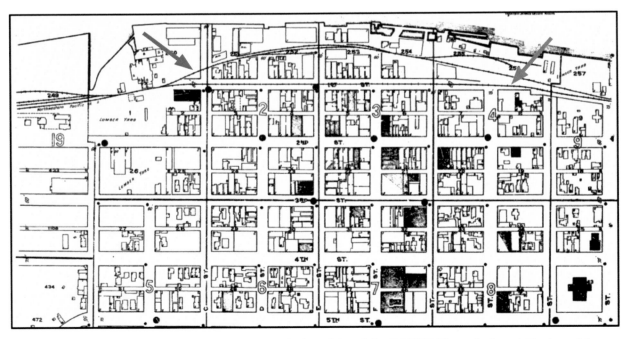

Figure 68: North Eureka, showing the C&N tracks (purple) and the E&KRRR's tracks (wine) (Sanborn Map Company 1920).

show that the steam shovel is making rapid advancement, and that the cut is closely approaching the highest point (78 feet) of the survey" (Fountain 2001:(50)88).

The E&KRRR, having built south from Arcata Junction, was approaching the northern end of Brainard's Point. Expenses would skyrocket if it had to cut through the point. It then suspended work and waited as the battle for the Eureka right-of-way was settled (Borden 1958:8).

On September 29 the C&N's cut at Brainard Point had reached a depth of 70 feet (Fountain 2001:(50)88). The right-of-way agreement was settled on October 9. The C&N finished its cut at Brainard's Point and on October 30 completed its line to Arcata (Borden 1963:10). For a mile north of Bracut the C&N's tracks were paralleled by the E&KRRR's unfinished railbed, which lay to the west of the C&N's and formed a sort of unintended breakwater on the bay (NWP 1917). Over time the E&KRRR's piling over Jacoby Creek and Gannon Slough deteriorated, leaving rotting reminders of the rail line that was never finished.

So it was that the E&KRRR never completed trackage between Eureka and Arcata. The C&N had finished theirs but never ran any trains on it. Instead, the C&N, which had no rolling stock of its own, leased their brand-new line to—who else?—the E&KRRR (Borden 1963:10). When the first E&KRRR train ran down the C&N's tracks, on December 14, 1901, it was a moment of high irony upon the steel rails.

Figure 69: Steam shovel cutting through Brainard's Point, 1900 (HSU Library).

Figure 70: Gannon Slough, 1947, with dikes, causeways, and roadways (HSU Library).

Other prospective railroads were formed but evaporated before ever laying track. One was A. B. Hammond's Humboldt Railroad, which hoped to build from Dyerville, in southern Humboldt County, to Crescent City (Carranco and Sorensen 1988:40). In May 1903, the big players began moving their rail line chess pieces around the board. On May 12, the Santa Fe incorporated the San Francisco & Northwestern Railway, which two days later purchased The Eel River & Eureka Railroad and then the Pacific Lumber Company Railroad a day later (Borden 1963:11).

The first blow in the final railroad fight had been struck. On May 18 the Southern Pacific responded by buying the E&KRRR and the Humboldt Railroad. The E&KRRR promptly became the Oregon & Eureka Railroad, was leased back to its former owners, and served to block the Santa Fe's expansion north from Eureka. The Santa Fe retaliated on July 7 by having the San Francisco & Northwestern acquire the California Midland, but since this line merely ran up the Van Duzen River, the purchase wasn't much of a counterpunch (Borden 1963a:11).

Both sides caught their breath. Then, on March 22, 1904, the San Francisco & Northwestern acquired, after a long wait, the C&N. Later that year a final agreement was reached on the waterfront trackage through Eureka, with various lines exchanging half-interests in segments of the tracks. Now the San Francisco & Northwestern, having absorbed the Pacific Lumber Company

Railroad, began laying track up the Eel River south of Scotia (Borden 1963:13). Its lodestone was San Francisco Bay.

Both the Santa Fe and the Southern Pacific were intent on reaching this destination. They both sent out surveying crews to determine the best route. Bill Hood, the Chief Engineer for the Southern Pacific, decided that going up the main Eel was the answer. Chief Engineer Bill Storey of the Santa Fe thought the South Fork was the preferable route (Kneiss 1956:133-134). The engineers filed their reports, which indicated that both ways would be highly expensive. So expensive, in fact, that neither rail line wanted to absorb the full cost. Decisions were made in each boardroom, and the result became apparent on November 24, 1906, when the Southern Pacific and the Santa Fe *jointly* formed the Northwestern Pacific Railway (Borden 1963:13). This new entity was in operation for less than two months while it cleared up "the financial problems of their properties." Then, on January 8, 1907, a new corporation with a slightly different name, the Northwestern Pacific Railroad (NWP), began operations. It immediately took over the San Francisco & Northwestern (Borden 1963:13).

Figure 71: Piling in Gannon Slough from the uncompleted railbed of the Eureka & Klamath River Railroad, 2009 (Gisela Rohde).

Figure 72: Cerise arrows show the Eureka & Klamath River Railroad's railbed near Bayside Cutoff (Humboldt County Public Works).

The NWP directors formed a committee to determine which route their railroad would take out of Humboldt County. On the committee Bill Hood and Bill Storey were joined by Bill Edes, the newly appointed Chief Engineer of the NWP. The three Bills reviewed the survey records and then spent several weeks with NWP personnel traveling by horseback, along with a pack train, through both river canyons. The committee then compared notes and decided that Bill Hood's route was best. The NWP would go up the main Eel (Kneiss 1956:133-134; Stindt and Dunscomb 1964:49).

When the NWP was incorporated in 1907 it enfolded several precursor rail lines that were already operating. The NWP's line north of Eureka became known as the Trinidad Branch, after what became the northernmost station on the route. Between Eureka and Arcata there were eventually several stations, stops, or junctions. Going north from Eureka Slough the first of these was Freshwater Junction, where the PL rail line from Freshwater met the NWP's tracks. There were stops at Brainard and Bracut (Stindt and Dunscomb 1964:91). Bayside station was at what became the western end of the Bayside Cutoff. The station was a flag stop where a mail sack was thrown off the train as it passed by. James Peter McRorie, with his wheelbarrow close at hand, waited for the sack to

Figure 73: Eureka-Arcata Limited at Jacoby Creek, 1948. Arrows show the outer linear fill prism for the Eureka &
Klamath River Railroad railbed, the fill closest to Arcata Bay (HSU Library).

land. He then placed it in the wheelbarrow and wheeled the "mailbarrow" along a plank boardwalk
that ran from the Bayside Station to the Bayside Post Office. The boardwalk paralleled Bayside Cutoff to Old Arcata Road, turned north, and then ran along the west side of the latter road to Bayside
(Schafran 1984:24; Fountain 2001:(23)65). Just south of Gannon Slough was Bayside Junction,
where a short section of track east of the main line connected the NWP with the Flanigan, Brosnan
and Company railroad (Stindt and Dunscomb 1964:91; Belcher Abstract & Title Co. 1922:7). It is
uncertain when this connection was constructed.

For a time the NWP ran north from Arcata all the way to Trinidad. The trackage diminished
in 1933, when the line between Korblex, north of Arcata, and Trinidad was abandoned (Rohde
2016:30). The northern portion of the NWP, including all of that in Humboldt County, went
through changes of ownership in the 1980s and the 1990s. It was officially closed by the Federal
Railroad Administration in 1998 (Wikipedia 2020a Mitchell 2020).

NWP mapping clearly indicates that the E&KRRR right-of-way lay west of the NWP tracks. It
also shows that both the NWP's and E&KRRR's right-of-ways cut through a portion of the levee
(dike) that ran between Gannon Slough and Jacoby Creek (NWP 1916a).

(Note: A detailed account of rail line right-of-way acquisitions from north Eureka to south Arcata
is attached to this report as an appendix.)

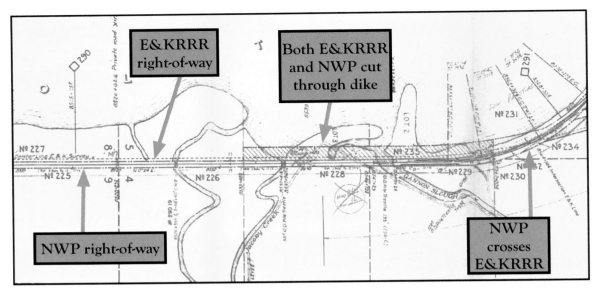

Figure 74: Location of NWP and E&KRRR rights-of-way and of Harpst & Spring dike, showing E&KRRR right-of-way closest to bay and showing that both rail lines cut through Harpst & Spring dike, with the rail line causeways forming new barriers (NWP 1916).

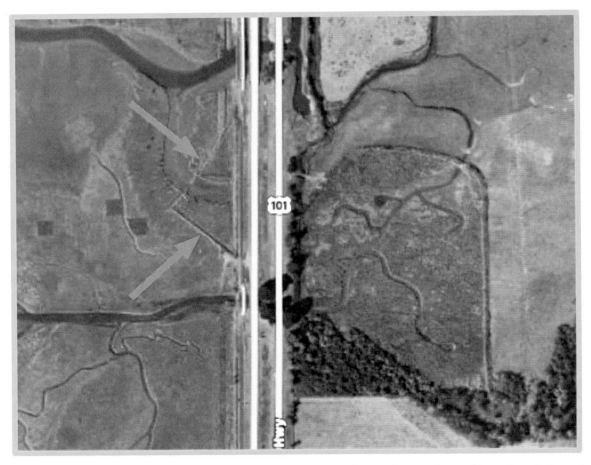

Figure 75: Orphan dike remnant between Gannon Slough and Jacoby Creek created by rail lines (aerial photo from Apple Maps 2020).

Figure 76: Current railroad bridge over Eureka Slough (Stock Schlueter).

D. Roads and Highways

1. First (1855) Eureka-Arcata Road

According to Dunbar Averill, writing in 1853, early day whites would use "an old Indian trail leading around the bay" if they wished to travel between Eureka and Union (Arcata) by horseback (Coy 1982:72). The Wiyot trail in that area ran "around the marsh on the east side of the bay" (Loud 1918:231). This was the route used by the Gregg Party in 1849 when they made their way south past Humboldt Bay (Lewis 1966:137-138).

Although some accounts (Coy 1982:74) claim that the first road between Eureka and Arcata was completed in 1862, there is evidence that an earlier wagon route was in place as early as 1855. In that year the Humboldt County Board of Supervisors indeed declared a road from Eureka to Arcata to be a public highway (Humboldt Times, May 16, 1855). While the declaration itself is not proof that such a road existed, a report from June 1855 confirms its presence:

> The Road Hence to Eureka—We are requested to call the attention of the Supervisors of the road hence to Eureka to the fact that the county road is fenced in and that parties living near the first slough this side

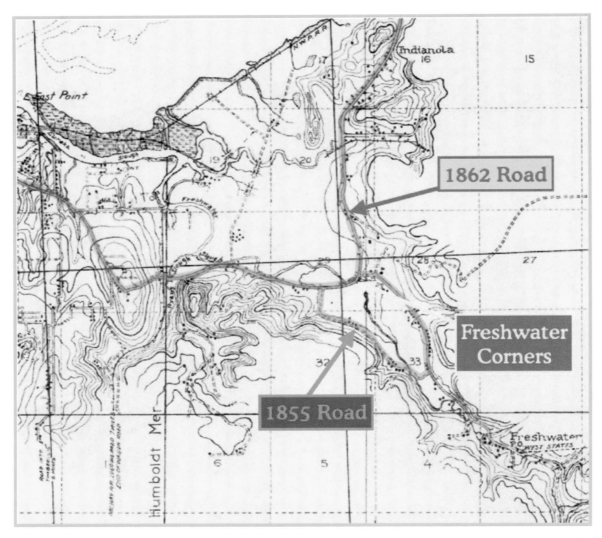

Figure 77: Route of 1855 Eureka-Arcata road around the Freshwater wetlands vs. 1862 Eureka-Arcata road on causeway through wetlands, which is now Myrtle Avenue (U.S. Army Corps of Engineers 1922).

of Eureka, have carried off a large portion of the planks from the bridge, rendering the road impassable (Humboldt Times, June 2, 1855).

The *Times* at the time was published in Union (Coy 1982:63), hence the phrase "the road hence [from Union] to Eureka."

In the Freshwater Corners area this 1855 road followed a distinctly different course from its 1862 successor, since it curved south to fully avoid the wetlands associated with Freshwater Slough. The slough drains a marsh that extended southerly all the way to the center of Section 33, Township 5 North, Range 1 East, Humboldt Meridian, which is about three-quarters of a mile south of the intersection of Myrtle Avenue with Freshwater Road. The causeway that carried the 1862 road (to-day's Myrtle Avenue) in front of Freshwater Farms was built on top of the wetland, thus avoiding the lengthy southward swing of the 1855 road. The 1862 causeway created what was probably the first dike in the Freshwater-Fay-Ryan slough area.

Jack Spear, who lived on Spear Road (now known as Jessica Lane), about halfway between Freshwater Corners and Freshwater, described the 1855 road in a circa-1948 interview on a local radio show called the "Old Timers' Program." Spear indicated that

> . . . the county road from the old Freshwater Tannery it didn't go where it now goes across the marsh. It went up pretty near the Ford [?] place right on the hill right going [across] the Ford Ranch. And it crossed the road where the Dick Hart place used to be and up right across where the Freshwater Pond is now and came out on the road where McCready lives. That was the road, the first I remember. That's the way we used to travel with wagons and teams. Then . . . it went up by our place, the Spear place (Spear 1948).

Spear next described the route of road as it then went north towards what later became Myrtle Avenue. He then talked about the road itself:

> The road from the tannery up to, well, in fact, clean up to the McCready Place it was what you called a corduroy road. It was laid out with alder poles and willow poles that [they] could get that lay across the road because the low ground was awful wet and kind of swampy. Had to keep something [?] cause the wagons would go out of sight, the wheels would go out of sight down in the mud. The horses would even get mired (Spear 1948).

Based on Spear's information, the 1855 road departed from the course of today's Myrtle Avenue about one-half mile west of Freshwater Farms, followed the southward indentation of Tannery Gulch and then ran southeast near the base of the hillside to Felt Road. There it ran on the course

Figure 78: Freshwater Corners area, 1947, showing various transportation routes (HSU Library).

of Felt Road to its end, on the former McCready property; crossed Freshwater Creek and went east on today's Thistle Lane; crossed Freshwater Road and continued east, probably on today's Brandon Lane; turned left near the eastern edge of the Freshwater Valley and ran north to meet the route of today's Myrtle Avenue. The 1922 Corps of Engineers map shows this route before the road crossing at Freshwater Creek was eliminated (United States Army Corps of Engineers 1922). Rusty Moore, a longtime resident of Redmond Road, also thought that the original road went farther inland because the area "was so swampy prior to dyking." Moore believed that Freshwater Creek was tidal up to Freshwater Stables, which is located on the site of Eddyville (Van Kirk 2006a:13).

2. Myrtle Avenue – Old Arcata Road

The 1855 Eureka-Arcata road apparently received little improvement after it was built. In 1859 the *Humboldt Times* expressed doubt "that a wagon road joining the two towns would ever be able to compete successfully with water communication, the reasons being given that the distance by land was about double that across the bay, and that the nature of the country made the construction and maintenance of a road very expensive" (Coy 1982:74).

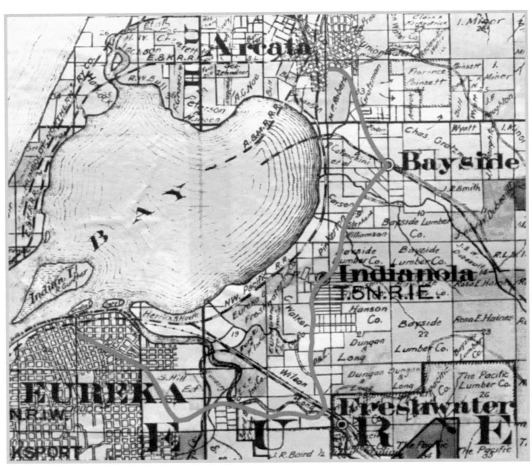

Figure 79: Eureka-Arcata road (in pink) in 1911 skirts most of the east Arcata Bay wetlands. It would take the coming of the bayside Redwood Highway to provide a much shorter, concrete-surfaced route (Denny 1911).

Figure 80: Eureka-Arcata road south of Bayside Cutoff showing Stephens family's curly redwood fence (Jack Irvine Collection).

Despite the *Times's* prediction, in May 1861 the Board of Supervisors directed the county road overseers to spend "at least two-thirds of their road taxes on the Arcata-Eureka road." The following month work had started on the Arcata end of the thoroughfare (Van Kirk 2007a:8). By June 22 the road was ready for use from Arcata south to Brainard Point. Work continued, but it was difficult going: "the heavy timber came so close to the marshlands that the road builders had to contend with both of these unfavorable elements and much attention was required to keep it in good repair" (Coy 1982:225).

Nonetheless, in August 1862 the *Humboldt Times* reported that "the road from this place [Eureka] to Arcata, around the Bay, which is now open, is a good piece of work." C. W. Long and J. Tracy took the first trip over the road and reported "that the drive can be made with ease in two hours and a quarter" (Humboldt Times, August 9, 1862). The route, as it was shown on Doolittle's 1865 county map, appears to generally follow the course of today's Myrtle Avenue and Old Arcata Road, although researcher Susie Van Kirk described places where it took "a more easterly route," noting that the "marshes shown on this map are far more extensive than today and in an effort to avoid them, the road overseers were willing to trade a little grade and a route in the trees for a drier road bed" (Doolittle 1865; Van Kirk 2007a:8). No mention is made however, of the causeway that was created between Tannery Gulch and Freshwater Corners, which allowed the new route to avoid the wide southern curve that the original road took to avoid the wetlands.

The narrow route between the dense redwood forest on the east and the marshlands to the west was frequently subject to afflictions induced by Nature. Even before the winter rains there were

Figure 81: Eureka-Arcata road, probably between Indianola and Bayside Cutoff (HSU Library).

complaints about the road in the late 1860s, with the *Times* claiming it was only a "tolerable summer road" at its best (Humboldt Times, May 15, 1869).

A stage run between Eureka and Arcata started in the summer of 1866, but it is hard to imagine that the passengers enjoyed the trip. A litany of complaints, ranging from "impassable" to "not safe for use," appeared in the *Times* during the late 1860s and early 1870s (Hedlund 1978:15). Once, in June 1870, there was some positive news when it was reported that "road overseer McLaughlin has made some good and substantial improvements" (Humboldt Times, June 4, 1870). The change was timely, for by August two stage lines were operating between Arcata and Eureka. George Conners, "an obliging and attentive gentleman," had the mail route, while Murphy and Simpson, who operated the Arcata Livery Stable, ran the other line (Humboldt Times, August 20, 1870). It was not impossible to think that at last there was a land route that would be preferable to taking the ferry across Arcata Bay.

But the bright spot of 1870 faded into the damp darkness of renewed roadbed deterioration, finally reaching a point in February 1876 when the road became impassable; travelers had to take the bay ferry *Gussie McAlpine* instead (Hedlund 1978:15).

Ironically, the road's quality was diminishing just as its importance increased. In 1873 the Eureka-Arcata road became the gateway to a new county road that was built from Freshwater Corners to the lower Kneeland area, following the course of today's Greenwood Heights Road (Humboldt

Times, November 29, 1873). The significance of the new route was enhanced when the road was subsequently extended through Kneeland's Prairie, Iaqua, Yager, Robinson's Crossing (later renamed Bridgeville), Blocksburg, Alderpoint, and Harris, before leaving Humboldt County and crossing over the Bell Springs Grade to reach destinations as far away as San Francisco Bay. The road was completed in 1877 (Rohde forthcoming).

The Eureka-Arcata road endured. The 1886, 1898, and 1911 official Humboldt County maps all show it as the only land route connecting Eureka with Arcata. The narrow lines on the 1911 map actually depicted a much improved version of the road, for in 1910 the Eureka and Freshwater Investment Company rebuilt the route from Bayside all the way to Ryan Slough. Several new bridges were constructed along the road and the *Humboldt Times* indicated that it now had "an excellent grade and a graveled surface" (Humboldt Times, February 26, 1910).

For decades the Eureka-Arcata road continued to serve as the only land connection between the two cities until the Redwood Highway was built over seven years, from 1918 to 1925 (Hedlund 1978:15). By 1922 the Bayside Cutoff provided a link between the Eureka-Arcata road and the new highway (Belcher Abstract & Title Co. 1922:7). And by 1933 the first route between Indianola and the highway was open (USGS 1933); it was superseded by the construction of the Indianola Cutoff in 1971. The only other connecting route between the highway and Eureka-Arcata road was the ranch road that ran across the Devoy property, the eastern end of which is now Devoy Road (Hed-

Figure 82; Eureka-Arcata road at Felt Road, flooded in 1922 by an overflowing Freshwater Slough (HSU Library).

lund 1978:15). Today the Eureka-Arcata road has two official names: south of Indianola it is part of Myrtle Avenue, while from Indianola north it is Old Arcata Road.

The completion of the Redwood Highway reduced the Eureka-Arcata road's status to that of a transportation link between a series of small, rural communities that includes Freshwater Corners, Freshwater, Indianola, and Bayside. Yet the road also serves the vital function of being an alternative to Highway 101 when that route is blocked by traffic problems or the whims of Nature. In the era of sea level rise, the road that was built around wetlands, rather than on top of them, may see increased use.

Figure 83: The old and the new at Freshwater Corners: powerful horses replaced by horsepower (HSU Library).

3. Private Roads

Most of the Eureka Slough system has been skirted by roadways, but three private roads have cut across the reclaimed wetlands. At the east end of Park Street, a private road crossed Freshwater Slough on a narrow bridge and then bore northeast to end near the site of Freshwater Landing. Devoy Road departs Myrtle Avenue as a county road, but north of the Devoy Ranch buildings a private road ran north-northeast, crossed Fay Slough, and divided to reach two ranch sites. The westernmost of the two branches now provides hiking access to the Fay Slough Wildlife Area from a trailhead just east of Harper Motors. Another private road departed Myrtle Avenue opposite the western end of Redmond Road; it headed southwest, crossed the Pacific Lumber Company Railroad grade, and then turned west to reach the Stephen Wilson barn. The west-running portion of this road is adjacent the southern boundary of the Wilson Ranch. At one time the Wilson family had extensive holdings on both sides of Myrtle Avenue (Denny 1911, Belcher Abstract & Title Co. 1922:7). Steven Wilson was born on the family ranch in 1871, a few years after his parents, Alexander and Jane Wilson, obtained the property. He died in 1954 (Humboldt Times, July 9, 1954). Rusty Moore, a longtime resident of Redmond Road, indicated that he had not seen any use of the ranch road for "years and years." He recalled that about 1960 a girl would get on the school bus at the ranch road (Moore 2020).

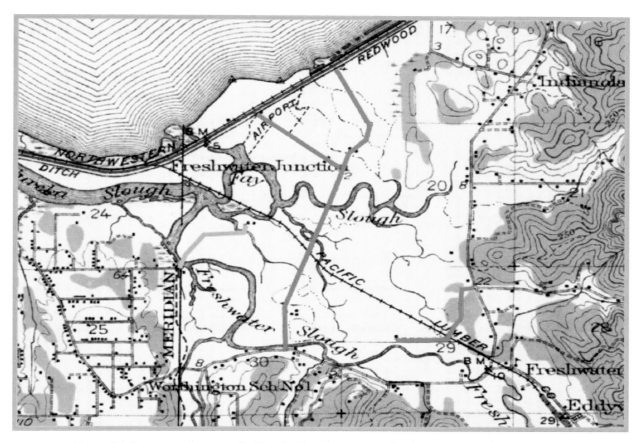

Figure 84: Private roads across the Eureka Slough system wetlands: orange, road to Freshwater Landing; lavender, Devoy Ranch roads; cerise, Stephen Wilson Ranch road (USGS 1942).

4. U. S. Highway 101

From the 1870s to the 1910s, the primary road connection between Humboldt County and areas to the south was rendered difficult and sometimes impassable by an obstacle in northern Mendocino County known as the Bell Springs grade, a section of mountainous roadway dreaded by travelers from the south for its 20-percent inclines and even more dreaded by travelers from the north for its 30-percent slopes. The development of the California highway system in the 1910s brought joy to North Coast travelers, as Highway Route One, from San Francisco via Crescent City to Oregon, replaced the Bell Springs grade with a section along the South Fork Eel whose incline never exceeds six percent. Another boon for motorists was the paving, with concrete, all the way from San Francisco Bay "to a few miles to the north of Eureka" (Blow 1920:60-61, 100). Those "few miles to the north" of course was the stretch between Eureka and Arcata.

Work on the Eureka-Arcata section of the highway started in 1918, with grading done by Mercer-Fraser Co. Rock surfacing by day labor was completed in 1921, followed by J. F. Knapp's company doing the paving in 1924. Day laborers then finished grading and added rock borders in 1925 (State of California Division of Highways 1928:171).

The state highway engineers were faced with a problem at Eureka Slough, since the waterway was frequented by boats and scows of varying dimensions that carried cargoes and passengers on the slough. The highway bridge there would have to accommodate this traffic. As the Highway Commission explained the solution,

Plate LXXXI. State Highway, Humboldt County, bridge across Eureka Slough, showing lift span open.

Figure 85: Lift-span state highway bridge over Eureka Slough, c. 1920 (State of California Highway Commission 1922:146).

Figure 86: A 1948 photo of the truncated Parker truss bridge (cerise arrow) that replaced the original lift span bridge for the highway crossing over Eureka Slough (HSU Library).

The Eureka Slough bridge, in Humboldt County, is interesting because of the use of a wooden lift span, made necessary on account of the lumber [sic] traffic on the slough. The total length of the bridge is 712 feet, made up of an east approach of sixteen 30-foot reinforced concrete piles: the lift span, above mentioned, 75 feet long, on concrete piers, with wood towers, and with creosoted pile fenders and dolphins; and a west approach of the same type as the eastern one, but of only four spans of 30 feet. The roadway is 21 feet wide, and the entire bridge is built over a salt marsh (California Highway Commission 1921:77). Mercer, Fraser Co. contracted to build the bridge on February 26, 1919 for a cost of $83,908 (State of California Division of Highways 1928:171).

Interesting the lift span may have been, but it was a cumbersome obstacle to the free flow of traffic across Eureka Slough. In a time when boats were still navigating the slough the lift span was subject to periodic raising and lowering, during which time vehicles on the highway were forced to stop, just as they had been until 1941 at Freshwater Junction, near Murray Field, where Pacific Lumber Company log trains would periodically cross the highway. So it was that in 1943 the aging, aggravating lift span was replaced by what can be described as a "truncated Parker truss" bridge (Bridgehunter.com 2020a; Evans 2020a).

In 1947 the Collier-Burns Act was signed into law by Governor Earl G. Warren. Thanks to the act, the California Division of Highways was "assured of approximately $76,000,000 yearly for new state highway construction." The legislation was funded by an increase in gasoline and diesel taxes

Figure 87: Traffic crowds Highway 101 on Arcata's G Street in the early 1950s (California Highways and Public Works 1953:2).

of 1 ½ cents per gallon and raising various vehicle and license fees. The goal, according to a state highways publication, was "to build more urgently needed multiple lane divided highways which will reduce California's excessively high traffic accident toll" (California Highways and Public Works 1947:1). The Collier-Burns Act is credited with creating the California freeway system and with providing a model for the subsequent interstate highway system that was initiated by the federal government in the 1950s (Mitchell 2020).

State Senator Randolph Collier was born in Etna, in Siskiyou County. He was the grandson of a former governor of Alabama. Collier "was elected as a Republican in 1938, but switched to the Democratic Party in 1959 when he opposed Senator William F. Knowland's campaign for the governorship" (New York Times, August 3, 1983). Assemblyman Michael J. Burns represented Del Norte, Humboldt, and Mendocino counties (onevoter.org 2020). He later died in office, while a state senator, in May 1949 (cahighways.org 2020).

In the early 1950s "traffic counts . . . [indicated] that the portion of the Redwood Highway, Route 101, between Eureka and Arcata was one of the most congested two-lane highways in the State of California." It was the time of the post-World War II housing boom, and log trucks, bound for the many nearby mills, crowded the existing highway.

To deal with the problem, state highway engineers developed an ambitious three-part project to convert the clogged section of two-lane highway to four-lane freeway (California Highways and Public Works 1953:1-2). In May 1954 work started on upgrading the highway, with a cloverleaf under construction north of Arcata at the intersection with Highway 299, and with a new bridge being built over Eureka Slough at the eastern edge of Eureka to accommodate the freeway's northbound traffic (JRP 2004:17). The new freeway was slated to have two lanes in each direction, with a 70-foot-wide median strip that allowed for the later construction of additional lanes. In September 1955 the section between Eureka and Arcata was dedicated as the Michael J. Burns Freeway to honor the co-author of the Collier-Burns Act. It marked the first time a freeway in California had been named for a person (Blue Lake Advocate, September 22, 1955). When the highway was widened in 1955, some 500,000 cubic yards of earth were removed from Brainard's Cut and used for fill on the expanded roadway (Fountain 2001:(104)270). At the conclusion of construction highway district engineer Alan Hart stated that

> The completion of the freeway fulfills a long-felt need in the matter of highway improvement in the Humboldt Bay area wherein traffic volumes, continually increasing from year to year, overtaxed the old, two-lane facility with resultant severe traffic congestion and delays. The sector of highway gains in importance wherein it serves as the major artery in the Humboldt Bay metropolitan area, the most densely populated area in extreme northwestern California. It is a prime example of a section of highway that is not only a portion of a main route carrying long-distance through traffic, but is also of vital importance to the local transportation needs, especially a "Main Street" between the cities of Eureka and Arcata, which are closely related in the daily activities of the area (Hart 1955).

Figure 88: Southern end of the Michael J. Burns Freeway, 1957, showing the four-lane roadway, two freeway bridges, the NWP pivot bridge, and business development along Jacobs Avenue (HSU Library).

IV. Diking and Reclamation of Tidelands

California was granted "swamp and overflowed" lands on September 28, 1850, less than three weeks after it had become a state. Some 2,192,456.70 acres of qualifying property were conveyed by the federal government; the lands could then be purchased from the state at $1.25 per acre. When proof was given that an equal amount of money had been spent on reclamation work the owner would be repaid his purchase price (Robinson 1948:191-193). Over time, almost 98% of Humboldt Bay's submerged and tide lands "have been filled or diked and reclaimed" (Laird 2005:5). On east Arcata Bay two sets of landowners did almost all of the reclaiming.

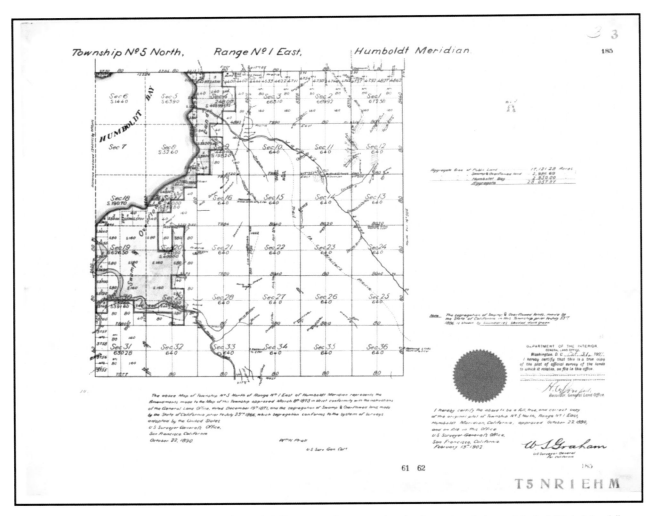

Figure 89: An 1890 revision of General Land Office map showing what had previously been labeled "Salt Marsh" as "Swamp & Overflowed Land" in township 5N, 1E, Humboldt Meridian. The change in terminology was necessary to allow the state to sell these lands, at a nominal price, rather than having them retained as state sovereign lands (U. S. Surveyor General's Office 1890a).

A. Bayside-Jacoby Creek Area

Diking to reclaim wetlands along the bay shore north of Jacoby Creek occurred in 1892. It was described in detail by the *Arcata Union*:

The Harpst & Spring Dike—It starts in on the bank of Butcher Slough just beyond the town line and follows the course of the slough as near as possible to the bay. Here it follows along the edge of the mudflats for a mile or more and crosses Flanigan and Brosnan's railroad at the edge of the bay. It then goes down along the bay, comes up and crosses the big slough [Gannon Slough] by the draw bridge where a flood gate will be put in, and follows down the further bank of the slough to the mouth of Jacoby Creek. From there it follows up the bank of the creek till it gets out of the reach of the highest tides and there ends.

The dike is ten feet wide at the base, 4 ½ feet at the top, and five feet high. . . . The dike, when finished, will be 400 rods long and will enclose about 350 acres of land. Of this land 115 acres belonged to the old Titlow place now owned by Harpst & Spring. Mel Roberts owns a part, Flanigan and Brosnan a part and Harpst & Spring, the remainder. . . .

The dike will be fenced along the inside and when finished will be a very large pasture.

The first owner who took up this marsh as swamp and overflowed land never dreamed that this large stretch of country, from Arcata to Jacoby Creek, inhabited only by the festive clam and the busy little crab would someday be pasture for hundreds of cattle. . . . The expense of building and the credit of inaugurating this fine piece of work was shared in alike by Flanigan & Brosnan and M.P. Roberts. (Arcata Union, June 18, 1892).

Figure 90: Arcata-Jacoby Creek diking machine, 1893 (HSU Library).

A year later the *Union* reviewed the local diking activity, extolling its benefits:

> Reclaiming Tide Lands—For many years residents of Arcata owned the tide lands adjoining the bay south of town, using them as an inferior pasture occasionally, but the salt water made the feed very inferior and the land, covered by the tide twice a day, served only as a breeding place for mosquitoes and was an eye sore as one approached the place by the railroad. But this is all in process of change. Over a year ago certain men in Arcata determined to redeem their marsh land if possible, and immediately commenced to dyke against the tide, beginning just east of the railroad embankment and working east to the place of M.P. Roberts, who joined with them. From Mr. Roberts' place the work was continued east to the railroad of Flanigan, Brosnan & Co., where a flood gate was put in, and from there further east, redeeming the tide lands of that firm. Altogether the levee is two miles long, ten feet wide at the bottom, and five feet wide on top. The cost was in the neighborhood of five dollars per rod.
>
> At the present time the dyke forms a most efficient barrier against the tide, thoroughly redeeming what would otherwise be valueless marsh land. The amount of land reclaimed is about 400 acres, which, at the present time—but little over a year from the time the dyke was completed—affords excellent pasturage for many head of cattle and horses as the fat stock on the ranch of M.P. Roberts, and of his neighbors, Messrs. Harpst & Spring abundantly prove. The land has not yet been seeded to clover, as there is still too much salt in it for the grass to grow luxuriantly, but here and there sprigs of clover are coming up showing that when the rains of another winter have done their part to clear the land of salt, that the land will be inferior to none on Arcata bottom in its ability to grow a strong crop of that grass. This is land worth in the beginning but a few bits an acre for inferior pasture, transformed in the course of a year to a valuable property, the equal, if not, the superior of any other for grass growing and crop raising purposes. (Arcata Union, August 18, 1893).

So it was that horses and cattle succeeded "the festive clam and the busy little crab."

When Harpst and Spring started a creamery in 1895 they fed their dairy cows clover from the reclaimed wetlands:

> The idea of utilizing marsh land for grass and clover producing pasture is new in this section, but the fact has been established to a certainty that no land on Arcata bottom produces better or richer pasture than the marsh land when once the salt water has been shut off from it. In proof of this, last year Harpst & Spring planted 20 acres in clover, simply scattering the seed upon the top of the ground, without either plowing or harrowing. Now the clover is well set, looks rank and fine, while the old marsh grass is dying out and is replaced by a growth of tender young grass mixed with the clover. The firm has now sown 300 acres more of dyked land to clover and expect to have pasture in another year, together with their upland fields, to keep 300 head of milch cows (Arcata Union, May 25, 1895).

In 1900 three Ferndale dairymen—Edward B. Carr, Philip Calanchini, and Silvio Comisto—bought about 400 acres from "Harpst & Spring and Flanigan & Brosnan," 300 acres of which were reclaimed land that had "been dyked for about eight years and makes as good pasture as bottom land. The greater part is seeded to Italian rye grass which with the wild clover which springs up when the salt water is taken off, makes fine feed" (Arcata Union, May 19, 1900). Since the three purchasers' last names all began with the letter "C" it was not surprising that the operation was named the C.C.C. or Three C Ranch. Later that year the new owners put up a house and barn on the property and tapped into four springs, the water work being done by the aptly named C. L. Bottle (Arcata Union, October 27, 1900). By the following year C. E. Sacchi had rented the Three C Ranch and was milking about 60 cows there (Arcata Union, April 20, 1901). All went well until the winter of 1906-1907, when the Jacoby Creek dike broke and the stream flooded part of Sacchi's pasture. He

Figure 91: "Break in levee . . . looking towards Sunny Brae near Bayside. . . " (HSU Library).

thereupon sued the Bayside Lumber Company "for damage to land from water and driftwood resulting from a log jam on Jacoby Creek breaking dyke" (Arcata Union, October 12, 1907).

According to the suit, the Bayside Lumber Company had "for many years" cut and logged timber from its lands on both sides of upper Jacoby Creek. This resulted in an accumulation of "great quantities of debris and refuse logs" being placed in, or left upon the banks of, upper Jacoby Creek. To prevent this accumulated material from being washed downstream and "running over and inundating the lands of lower riparian owners," the company "caused to be formed . . . an immense jam and obstruction in and across Jacoby creek." This obstruction was some 400 yards long and ran from bank to bank. In 1905 the lumber company contracted with a shingle maker to remove timber from the obstruction and convert the wood into shingle bolts. When this was done, the jam was loosened to the extent that part of the remaining material flowed downstream. Some of this material lodged around one of the railroad trestles of the lumber company's railroad at a point opposite Sacchi's dike. The rains from the 1906-1907 winter caused the water from this new jam to back up and then break through Sacchi's dike, flooding about eighty acres of Sacchi's pasture and forming a new creek channel through the ranch land. Repairing the damage would take an estimated two years, which coincided with the length of Sacchi's lease. The jury hearing the case awarded Sacchi $3,500 in damages (Casetext 2020), which would be equivalent to about $98,505 today (measuringworth.com 2020b).

The Bayside Lumber Company appealed the decision. In April 1910, the California Court of Appeals upheld the verdict in favor of Sacchi (Arcata Union, April 2, 1910). Later that year he "secured another eight year lease on the ranch" (Arcata Union, September 10, 1910). Sacchi was still leasing the ranch in 1918 when the property was "being tiled for draining" (Arcata Union, February 28, 1918). Finally, in March 1920, Sacchi ended his relationship with the Three C Ranch when he sold his lease on the property for $41,500, "the record price for the year" (Arcata Union March 18, 1920). The income that Sacchi derived from this sale would, a century later, have a value of about $530,956 (measuingworth.com 2020a), enough for most people to retire on and probably enough to make them believe that land reclamation was worthwhile.

Picture #2. Looking East, Showing Waste to right.

Figure 92: Court exhibit in Sacchi vs. Bayside Lumber Co. showing material in upper Jacoby Creek (Jack Irvine Collection).

Picture "11. Looking South up Rapids.

Figure 93: Court exhibit in Sacchi vs. Bayside Lumber Co. showing logging debris in upper Jacoby Creek (Jack Irvine Collection).

B. Freshwater Slough-Fay Slough Area

Dr. Reuben Gross, a Eureka physician, his wife Mary, and John A. Sinclair, a superintendent at the Pacific Lumber Company mill in Scotia, purchased over a thousand acres of Swamp and Overflowed Land in 1889 from two mill owners who had been partners in the Excelsior Redwood Company, C. A. Hooper and David Evans. The parcels included most of the Fay Slough and Freshwater Slough drainages along with a shoreline strip that ran from west of Walker Point to the southern end of Brainard's Point (Van Kirk 2007a:12).

Preparatory to diking these wetlands, Reuben Gross purchased the dredger that Harpst and Spring had used to dike their wetlands at Bayside (Arcata Union, May 25, 1895). In the Fay Slough area the first dikes were built from "about midway between Bayside Cutoff and Indianola Road down to perhaps where the eucalyptus trees are along Highway 101 with another piece of dike following along the northern edge of Fay Slough beginning in the west half of section 20 and extending into the northwest quarter [of] section 19" (Van Kirk 2007a:12).

The *Humboldt Times*, referring to what the *Arcata Union* had termed a "dredger," called the same piece of equipment a "dyking machine." In December 1896 the *Union* summarized an article in the *Times* by stating that "the dyking machine . . . will soon be converted into a steam shovel." Gross and Sinclair were finished diking and their machine was sold to the Pacific Lumber Company (Arcata Union, December 12, 1896). By 1898 it was reported that the "Freshwater Reclamation District . . .

Figure 94: Devoy Ranch, west of Freshwater Slough, 1901. Walker Point in distance, right (Times Publishing Co. 1902:93).

Figure 95: Wheat threshing, probably on Freshwater Investment Company farmland, c. 1910 (author's collection).

extends with little interruption from Freshwater Slough on the south to Brainard's Point on the north and from the county [Eureka-Arcata] road to the bay shore and includes about 1200 acres" (Ferndale Enterprise, October 4, 1898).

Gross and Sinclair leased their tract to George and Henry Hanson in 1899. The property consisted of "1,000 acres enclosed by three separate dikes, creating three separate enclosures" (Van Kirk 2007a:19). That same year George Hanson built a creamery on the Walker Point portion of the property (Arcata Union, March 16, 1901).

The Gross & Sinclair tract was considered by the *Daily Humboldt Standard* to be "one of the finest pieces of land for dairying and stock raising in northern Humboldt" (Daily Humboldt Standard, November 9, 1899). Perhaps because of this evaluation, Albert C. Noe and D. W. Hanson purchased the 1100-acre property from Gross, Sinclair and their wives in 1905 and "immediately formed the Eureka and Freshwater Investment Company and sold their 1100-acre holding to the company in 1906 (Miller and McMorris 2018:19). The new owners subsequently rejected offers of double that amount, stating that "with the passage of every year the land, once mere mud flats, is growing more valuable for agricultural and dairying purposes" (Humboldt Times, December 22, 1908; Van Kirk 2007a:20). The Freshwater Investment Company's ranch produced a truly "splendid output" when in four days over 10,000 bushels of grain were harvested, weighing 160 tons (Humboldt *Times* 11 Sept. 1908; Van Kirk 2007a:20).

The grain grew, the potential of the property was recognized, and finally the Freshwater Investment Company received an offer it couldn't refuse. In 1914 the entire parcel was sold to "local businessman, rancher, and dairyman Henry M. Devoy" (Miller and McMorris 2018:19). About the same time the purchaser was lauded as an outstanding agriculturalist: "Such men as Henry DeVoy [sic]

Figure 96: Drawbridge over Freshwater Slough near Myrtle Avenue (HSU Library).

soon saw the great advantage of our [Humboldt County's] climatic conditions and scores of them have reaped fortunes from the soil" (Irvine 1915:148).

The property then became known as the Devoy Ranch. John Brazil leased 312 acres of what was called the "Freshwater Marsh" from Devoy. The land included part of Ryan Slough and its southern boundary was at Myrtle Avenue. There it was reported that Brazil,

> . . . with the aid of his sons . . . is operating one of the largest dairies in the county, milking one hundred thirty-five cows during the season. The herd is of high grade stock, the animals having been carefully selected for their yield of rich milk. . . . The ranch is all bottom land, which gives Mr. Brazil not only ample pasture, but an abundance of green feed for his herd of cows (Irvine 126-122).

By 1949 the Devoy Ranch had been split into several holdings. Members of the Devoy family still owned the parcel south of Fay Slough, Charles and Dorothy East owned the northwestern part of the Devoys former property, and the northeastern section was held by C. E. Hunt, F. and K. Layton, and Charles C. Falk Jr. (Metsker 1949:33).

A portion of the former Devoy Ranch became government property when the State of California acquired the c. 350-acre Mid-City Ranch in 1987. The following year the parcel was designated the Fay Slough Wildlife Area by the Fish and Game Commission. In 1989 an adjacent c. 150-acre ranch parcel was purchased and added to the wildlife area (wildlife.ca.gov 2020). These lands encompass

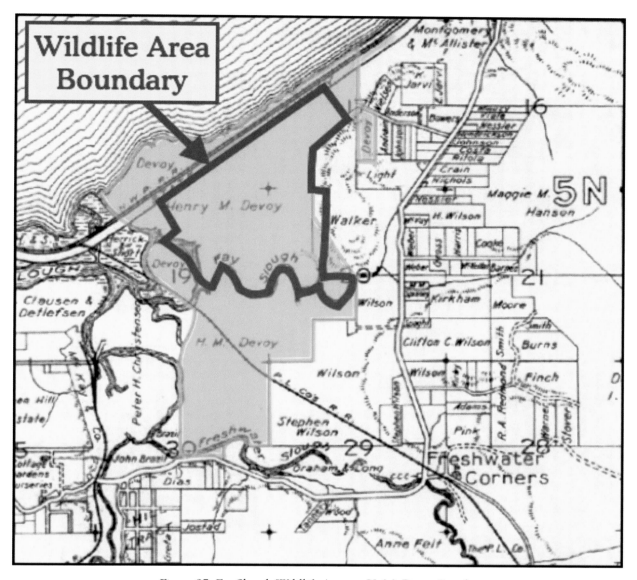

Figure 97: Fay Slough Wildlife Area vs. H. M. Devoy Ranch.

about 44 percent of former Devoy Ranch, which totaled about 1,100 acres. The wildlife area runs from Fay Slough north to the Highway 101 corridor.

C. Mudflat Sculpture Gallery

In the early 1970s the mudflats across Highway 101 from Murray Field were "reclaimed" by a group of anonymous artists, who "built a driftwood sculpture of Jesus." It was quickly torn down by another group who considered the sculpture sacrilegious. A *Times-Standard* editorial complained about an act of "needless vandalism," and the artists were soon back at work, their new creations left undisturbed. Peter Brant and some friends constructed a long, spiky dragon that appeared to have come out of the bay and was pausing before crossing the freeway. For years it served as a sort of centerpiece of the mudflat gallery, which also featured renderings of more likely residents of the area—boats, whales, and shorebirds (Sommer 2006).

For years the creations of gray-brown wood delighted motorists as they approached Eureka from Arcata. Many a driver would slow and look hopefully for additions to the gallery, and they were often gratified to find a new construction of recycled flotsam that brought a smile and perhaps an improved attitude as they entered the city on their way to work.

One day in 1986 they saw an especially dramatic sight—a driftwood airplane, its nose smashed down in the mud—crashed before it could make it to the nearby airport. It was the work of local muralist Duane Flatmo, and it had an unexpected consequence—a group of local pilots, who thought the sculpture might bring bad luck, "ripped it to shreds" (Doran 2006).

Flatmo rebuilt the plane. Again it was torn apart, and this time a threatening note was left among the debris. The incidents sparked a slew of letters to the editor. Even Flatmo agreed there was a problem, saying "it did get out of hand. It wasn't just my thing; there were tons going up out there. It had become a place to make political statements, and it got kind of trashy—along with the real sculptures. They hauled them all away" (Doran 2006).

And no dragons have been seen on the mudflats since.

Figure 98: The Dragon (North Coast Journal)

V. Business Developments

A. Brickyards on Eureka Slough

The presence of high quality clay near the bluff on the south side of Eureka Slough enabled the establishment of two brickyards in the vicinity. The longest lived was located a short distance northeast of the eastern end of Essex Street in Myrtletown; it operated for 90 years. In 1864 John B. Hill started his brick manufacturing plant on four acres there. The clay for the bricks was "dug from the banks of Eureka Slough." (California Bricks 2009a:1). Hill sold his business to James D. Thompson, J. Frank Zane, and John Porter in 1905, and they formed the Eureka Brick and Tile Company. Thompson had previously run a brick and tile plant in Fortuna. The brickmaking plant was located east of the clay pit; it had a capacity of 1,000,000 bricks per year, which was increased to 3,000,000 by 1915. Usually the output ran to about 50 per cent of capacity. The company's products included "common and pressed brick, hollow tile, and drain tile." Thompson bought out his partners in 1920, and accordingly changed the business's name to the Thompson Brick & Tile Company. In 1926 it became the J. D. Thompson Brick Company, perhaps indicating a discontinuation of tile making. (California Bricks 2009b:1-2). The clay pit's location proved convenient, since the Thompson Brick Company used a wharf that extended northward from their property on the south side of Eureka Slough from which to transport their bricks (Dietrich 1928:81). An account from 1928 describes the J. D. Thompson brickmaking process:

Figure 99: Pressed brick from Eureka Brick & Tile Company (California Bricks).

Figure 100: J. D. Thompson Brick Company (Deitrich 1928).

The clay is mined from an open pit with a Fordson tractor and a Fresno scraper. The pit has a maximum depth of 12 ft., but good clay is known to extend to greater depths. The clay bed is made up of irregular streaks of yellow, gray and black clay, with a varying proportion of sand. It is generally too plastic to be successfully used alone, and is mixed in the plant with a maximum of 15% of sand. The clay is dumped from the scraper into a hopper and from there it is elevated to the head of the plant in cars drawn by a cable hoist. . . .

In the plant, the clay is passed through a disintegrator, followed by a pug-mill and a Brevan auger machine equipped with a wire-cutter. The brick or tile are air-dried under sheds. In the cool, moist atmosphere of the locality, drying often requires a period of four weeks, and is seldom completed in less than two weeks.

Firing is done in a 30-ft. round down-draft kiln, which has a capacity of 75,000 brick or the equivalent volume of tile. The water smoking is done with wood, for a period of 75 hours. The burn is finished with oil, atomized with steam, requiring 75 hours additional. The finishing temperature is 1850° F.

The machinery is operated by steam power, generated in oil-fired boilers (Deitrich 1928:81-82).

The Thompson plant operated intermittently until Lorine and Henry Hindley bought the property after World War II. They ran the brickyard for about 10 years, until a big earthquake near Christmastime in 1954 destroyed much of the brickyard equipment. The Hindleys conducted one last firing of green brick and then shut the operation down. In 2009 Lorine Hindley, then 96, still owned the brickyard property. The one-story office building (of course made of brick) was remodeled and served as a rental house. The only other remains of the brickyard are foundations from the kilns, which are covered in berry vines (Renzullo 2009; Hindley and Klingenspor 2009).

Figure 101: J. D. Thompson Brick & Tile Company brickworks (note the hollow tiles in front of the water tank), looking west down Eureka Slough (HSU Library).

The second brick yard was about two hundred yards east of the Hindley brick works, at the north end of Marsh Road. According to one source, the Humboldt Clay Manufacturing Company was established there "around 1910" by Harrison M. Mercer, of the local Mercer-Fraser Company. The "clay was mined on Ryan Slough [*sic*], east of Eureka on 1 ¾ acres of land. . . . This company

Figure 102: Brickyard sites on lower Eureka Slough, with Park Street in foreground, Jacobs Avenue in background, 1954 (HSU Library).

Figure 103: Former office, Hindley Clay Products (Jerry Rohde).

manufactured sand-molded common brick until 1913, when the plant closed. In 1910 the bricks were used in the post office and court house on the corner of H and 5th streets, Eureka" (California Bricks 2009c).

A State Mining Bureau report provided the following information about this brick yard:

> *Humboldt Clay Manufacturing Company.* Lewis H. Hess, president, and W. Ernest Dickson, secretary, of Eureka. They own 1 ¾ acres of clay land adjoining the Eureka Brick and Tile Company in the suburbs of Eureka. The plant consists of one American Clay Machinery Company clay machine, one mixing machine, one disintegrator, one re-press, one cut-off machine, one 100 horsepower engine, two boilers, one oil tank (500 barrels). They sell the brick at $10 per 1000 at the yard and have a capacity of 25,000 brick a day" (Lowell 1915:22).

The Humboldt Clay Manufacturing Company is listed in the 1913 Eureka City Directory as having its office at 635 Third Street in Eureka (Polk-Husted 1913:71). Owner Lewis Hess died in 1957. He had also been "the owner of the Hess Fuel and Building Material Company of Eureka" (Fountain 2001:(25):460).

B. Jacobs Avenue

Between the mouth of Eureka Slough and Murray Field there lies a peninsula of marshland bounded by the slough on the south and Arcata Bay on the north. Over time it was bisected by the NWP rail line and the Redwood Highway, and the land south of the highway was diked. In the 1940s the land between the highway and Eureka Slough was owned by Harold and Louise Hilfiker (Metsker 1949:20). Harold was the owner of Hilfiker Concrete and Tile Works that was located in the Bucksport area, and which had been founded by his father, John, in 1902 (Hilfiker 2015:28).

Development of the Hilfiker parcel began in 1948. An aerial photo from that August shows a partly constructed facility labeled the "Eureka Auction Yards" at the east end of this peninsula, immediately west of the abandoned Pacific Lumber Company's rail line, beyond which is Murray Field. This was the year and place that

> Carl Johnson opened a lively and entertaining livestock auction as a way to market cattle to buyers. Carl knew that auctions were the best method for fair market value, which proved beneficial for both his company and his community. He never intended to expand his livestock auctions, but his entrepreneurial spirit drove him to expand his business much more throughout the years.

Figure 104: Lower Eureka Slough area, 1937, showing dike along northern side of slough (purple arrow) that protects the future site of Jacobs Avenue, and the undiked area north of Highway 101 (green arrow) that remains wetland (Humboldt County Public Works)

Figure 105: Western Eureka Slough, 1937 (Humboldt County Public Works).

> After he delivered cattle to the Bay Area, Carl realized he could load up his truck and haul something back to Humboldt to sell. And so the furniture and appliance departments were born. (carljohnsonco.com).

And, as the Carl Johnson Company's website tells it, the business kept expanding, as generation after generation of the Johnson family continued to conduct auctions and run the different segments of their operation, the company still firmly anchored at the eastern end of Jacobs Avenue (carljohnsonco.com).

By 1957 there was enough development along Jacobs Avenue that parts of two pages in that year's Sanborn insurance map set showed the various businesses. Starting with the Carl Johnson Co. on the east, there were, in westward progression: a trailer park, truck repair shop, auto painting shop, a contractor's storage and woodworking building, a tractor sales and parts business, a small office surrounded by a big empty lot, an auto wrecking yard and auto parts store, another small office and big lot, and a truck sales and service business (Sanborn Map Company 1957:87-88). Development continued until a full row of businesses filled the south side of Jacobs Avenue. Today, anyone kayaking on Eureka Slough will see a variety of surfaces along the slough's north bank—these represent the different methods of dike maintenance of the individual land owners on Jacobs Avenue, whose properties all run southward to the slough.

Figure 106: Carl Johnson Auction Yard under construction near Murray
Field, 1948, with log booms in the adjacent slough (HSU Library).

Figure 107: West end of Jacobs Avenue, 1954, showing auto wrecking business, center right
(HSU Library).

C. Murray Field

Early aviation in Humboldt County is closely linked with pilot Dayton Murray Sr. and with the wetlands east of Eureka. In August 1919 Murray "first winged into Eureka," landing his

> . . . wire-wheeled plane . . . in a grassy field north of the Cottage Garden nurseries in the Worthington district. . . . Murray used the field for about two years, then secured a site on the Charles Crivelli ranch beyond the defunct McKay shingle mill past the end of Park Street. When the highway to Arcata was completed about 1923, Murray secured a field a half-mile past the present one (Humboldt Standard, 20 October 1959).

This airstrip, which another source indicates was "established in the early 1920s," (Dreyer 1990:3) became known as Murray Field. The location of this original Murray Field was described by Elwain Dreyer, the son of early day pilot Charlie Dreyer, as follows:

> The airport was a piece of land carved out of the marsh of the Devoy Ranch. The entrance to the airport was from Highway 101, which was then a two-lane road between Eureka and Arcata. The entrance was at the present entrance to the Harper auto dealership, and the main part of the airport was just a little north of that road (Dreyer 1990:3).

Figure 108: First Murray Field, 1927 (Humboldt County Public Works).

Although Murray had stopped flying by the 1930s, he "helped persuade the Board of Supervisors to purchase a piece of land for an airport. The property was owned by Murray's uncle, Gilogy [sic], the price was $6,150.50" (Crichton 1984:5). A tract of 131 acres was purchased from the Henry Devoy Ranch, which was then owned by Mrs. Henry Devoy and her son-in-law, M. L. Gillogly (Fountain 1967:(29)18-19). Previously, the airport parcel had been owned by Herrick and Short (Belcher 1922:7). The Fortuna Businessmen's Association, perhaps hoping that the airport would be sited nearer their town, complained that "the land was subject to inundation and that after an expenditure of a large sum of county money, it would continue to be a mudhole and eventually be abandoned as an airport" (Fountain 1967:vol. 29:118). Despite this objection, the mudhole was approved as the site for the county airport by Humboldt County Planning Commission in June 1930. An alternative proposal by Mrs. Humboldt Gates, owner of Indian Island, to sell her property for $75,000, was rejected. It was noted that the island suffered the deficiencies of "being inaccessible to automobiles and that much of it is under water for a considerable portion of the year" (Humboldt Times, June 7, 1930). The Devoy-Gillogly land was finally purchased in 1934 (Humboldt Standard, December 9, 1935) after some haggling over the price with Gillogly (Fountain 1967:(29)19).

FIgure 109: First Murray Field, 1937, shortly before the move south to second Murray Field (Humboldt County Public Works).

Work on the new airport was reported as set to "begin before July 1 [1935] on filling gullies and ditches and general drainage" (Humboldt Standard June 20, 1935). Less than a year later, another article announced "virtual completion of the new county airport on the old Herrick tract, just south of the privately operated Murray Field" (Humboldt Times, April 19, 1936). The same news story indicated that "it may take some time, for settling and packing, before the new airport is ready for its first planes," and that "two bridges will be built soon to give access to the airport from the Redwood Highway."

In August 1937 the *Humboldt Times* announced that:

PLANS FOR NEW

HANGAR AT AIR

PORT FINISHED

East Ranch

Murray Field

Freshwater
Landing

Log Booms

Road to east end of Park St.

Figure 110: Murray Field, 1947, and other points of interest (HSU Library).

It was indicated that the plans for the hangar, which will cost approximately $10,000, were acceptable to the [county board of] supervisors.

According to architect [Frank T.] Georgeson, the hangar will be 85 feet wide and 60 feet deep. In addition there will be a shop or repair room.

The hangar will be sufficiently large to house from four to eight airplanes, depending on their size.

Eight doors, working on a rail as one door, will open the building, which will face northward. There will be a 15 foot clearance at the entrance, enabling a good sized plane to enter (Humboldt Times August 11, 1937).

Les Pierce, of Pierce Bros. Flying Service, indicated that after the hangar was built "I made arrangements to rent it for $30 a month, manage the airport, and be aviation advisor to the supervisors." (Dreyer 1990:5) Pierce added that:

Before getting much use out of the property as an airport, we had to do some work. Low spots were filled and we had to sandbag the dykes to keep the water from flooding at high tide. We pulled a drag behind my car to smooth out an airstrip and hand dug two ditches from the highway for phone and gas lines (Dreyer 1990:6).

Following the attack on Pearl Harbor in December 1941, a civil defense zone was instituted

Figure 111: Murray Field (green arrow) and Jacobs Avenue (purple arrow), 1960 (Humboldt County Public Works).

FIgure 112: The Pacific Lumber Company Railroad causeway forms most of the barrier between Murray Field and Eureka Slough. Here, where there was a trestle (still visible in the water) instead of a causeway, a section of dike was built to fill the gap (Aldaron Laird).

along a 100-mile-wide strip of the coast (Crichton 1984:6). At the time, "there were eight planes based at the airport. The next day all civilian flying was banned, and silence settled over the field" (Humboldt Times, January 30, 1949). On May 16, 1945, the airport reopened with two planes. By January 1949, there were 40 planes based at the airport, with both Pierce Flying Service and Fleming Flying Service operating there (Humboldt Times, January 30, 1949). In October 1959, the county airfield was dedicated as Murray Field to honor Dayton Murray Sr. (Dreyer 1990:7).

D. Brainard

Henry M. Devoy, who owned the 1,100-acre Devoy Ranch that stretched across much of the Fay Slough and Freshwater Slough wetlands, at various times leased parts of his property to other ranchers. The northern end of his ranch contained a 78-acre section that was separated from the rest of Devoy's land by the NWP's tracks and later by the state highway. This small parcel was rented out as a dairy operation. In 1921 Devoy and his son-in-law, Lee Gillogly, had a long row of eucalyptus trees planted on the rental property; the trees were adjacent the highway and were intended to serve as a windbreak (Times-Standard, March 16, 2018). The trees came from Cottage Garden Nurseries in Myrtletown; they were transplanted on the Devoy property by Jessie M. Nash, a worker at Cottage Garden (Nash 1996:41). Devoy reportedly failed to obtain permission from the state highway commission to plant the trees, which were in the highway corridor. The commissioners then threatened to remove the trees, but before they could take action a new group of apparently pro-eucalyptus commissioners was appointed and the trees were spared (Dillion 2008:A8). A hard freeze in 1933 devastated the temperature sensitive eucalyptus; they were cut down to stumps but they subsequently grew back. In 2008 plans were made to cut about half of the estimated 600 trees (Dillion 2008:A-8). Proposals for removing the trees have continued since then, always sparking controversy.

The Devoy family sold the ranch in 1943 to Charles L. East and Dorothy N. East (Miller and McMorris 2018:21). In 1947 the Easts sold a portion of the property to the Arcata Redwood Company (ARCO). The company's president, Howard A. Libbey, had operated a lumber mill and retail yard in Arcata since 1939. The new ARCO property was located at the edge of Humboldt Bay on a protrusion of land that was directly northwest of the NWP rail line and Highway 101. The location

Figure 113: Row of six-year-old eucalyptus trees between highway and rented dairy ranch, 1927 (Humboldt County Public Works).

Figure 114: Double row of eucalyptus stumps, 1933 (Humboldt County Public Works).

Figure 115: Thirty-year-old eucalyptus trees on the highway corridor c. 1964 (eurekahistory.com).

came to be called the "Brainard yard," or simply "Brainard," even though it was a mile southwest of Brainard's Point. ARCO's initial construction work at the site was completed in 1952. The facility was used for drying lumber cut at ARCO's Arcata mill and also to remanufacture smaller pieces of cut wood into a variety of products. Between 1954 and 1957 the dairy buildings from the former ranch were demolished and the drying yard expanded. In 1958 and 1960 additional land was reclaimed on the north and east sides of the parcel. By 1960 ARCO had built two mills north of Orick and had then closed its Arcata mill. Over time more buildings were added at the Brainard facility and the western portion of the property was paved over to expand the drying yard. (Miller and McMorris 2018:21-23; Carranco 1982:160-161).

ARCO was purchased by Simpson Timber Company in 1988. In 2006 Green Diamond split from Simpson Timber and formed the California Redwood Company (CRC), using the name of the earlier company that had held property in the Freshwater area. The new company merged with Samoa Properties and Arcata Redwood LLC in 2013. The former ARCO remanufacturing plant then became known as the CRC. In 2014 Green Diamond closed the plant and sold off the remaining lumber stock (Miller and McMorris 2018:34-35).

Figure 116: Former ARCO and CRC mill site (orange arrow), showing blockage of sloughs by the railroad and highway corridors (aerial photo from Apple Maps 2020).

E. Tannery

J. M. Sass started a tannery about a mile west of Freshwater Corners in early 1889. Sass explained that:

> Freshwater was selected as the location, first on account of the water, which is abundant and the very best in the county for tanning purposes. Second, on account of the shipping facilities afforded by Freshwater slough, which empties into the bay. Third, the location is central to large bodies of tan bark oaks in summer (Weekly Humboldt Standard, March 7, 1889).

The tannery included a building "to hold 800 cords of tanbark." The production capacity was "5000 hides a year" (Weekly Humboldt Standard, March 7, 1889). The tannery occupied a parallelogram-shaped property; one short side fit flush with the Eureka-Arcata road and the two long sides ran above a small declivity known as Tannery Gulch, which supplied the water necessary for the tanning process (Belcher Abstract & Title Co. 1922:7; Spear 1948). The tannery specialized in producing sturdy leather that was used for harnesses, horse collars, and similar products (Shoe & Leather Reporter 1919:727; Farmer 2014).

Sass had financial difficulties in the 1890s and the tannery went into receivership. In 1899 John

Figure 117: McCabe & Duprey Tannery (Humboldt County Historical Society).

Figure 118: Tannery Gulch, c. 2014 (Jerry Rohde).

Davis, Peter McCabe, and A. Duprey purchased the business (Arcata Union, May 20, 1899). In 1916 McCabe took over full control of the tannery (Farmer 2014).

According to Ruth McCabe Farmer, who observed the tannery as child, the "buildings were huge, the walls were corrugated iron." A structure at the rear of the property was used for grinding the tanoak bark, where there were also "huge redwood tanks" in which the bark was soaked in water. The big building near the Eureka-Arcata road was divided in half—one side contained the "wet tanks" wherein the hides soaked for four months in the tannin-rich liquid that had percolated in the redwood tanks; the other side of the ground floor had other equipment and a work area for a cobbler. An elevator took the wet hides to the building's second floor, which was used as a drying area (Farmer 2014).

McCabe bought tanoak-rich property at Maple Creek and Crother's Cove (now part of Prairie Creek Redwoods State Park) to provide a steady supply of tanbark. He was killed in an auto accident in 1927 and left his wife Alice with a $50,000 mortgage on the tannery and the tanoak properties. That was the end of the tannery, as Alice sold most of the holdings to pay off the debt. For a time she rented out the former tannery cookhouse for the income (Farmer 2014).

Today there are no remnants of the tannery buildings, which were burned in the 1940s (Humboldt Times, October 19, 1947). The gulch is still there—it served as the tannery's source of water and probably also as a disposal system that sent residue from the tanning process into Freshwater Slough. Now, however, that water is partly impounded by a pond that enhances what has become a residential property.

F. Midway Drive-In

In 1951 the Midway Drive-In theater began operation a short distance southeast of the junction of Highway 101 with Indianola Road. It had a capacity of 450 cars. The parking area was built on the bayside wetland. An oblique aerial photo from 1952 shows that the parking area has covered over the upstream end of a small slough. The Midway closed in September 1986 and is now used as a storage area for recreational vehicles. (Cinema Treasures 2020). A parcel between the drive-in and Highway 101 was developed for businesses. It currently houses a Smart Foodservice warehouse

Figure 119: Midway Drive-In, 1952 (HSU Library).

G. Bracut

Brainard's Point, the fishhook-shaped ridge that divided the Bayside wetlands from the Eureka Slough wetlands, was named for W. A. Brainard, who owned a tract of land that stretched from near the mouth of Jacoby Creek to the north end of Indianola. In 1878 he wrote to the *West Coast Signal* about his Humboldt County days, some 23 years after he had left:

In the year 1853 we lived in Humboldt County, California. We were engaged in lumbering and our camp was in the unbroken forest some seven miles from Eureka. We cut the lofty pines [Douglas-fir], magnificent spruce and majestic redwoods upon the plateau, hauled the logs with oxen, attached to a primitive timber truck, to the brow of a hill, where, with a sluice, we ran them into a small creek the emptied into the Bay (Brainard 1965:9).

It is likely that his logs entered the bay via Brainard's Slough, as he owned the slough and the lower course of Rocky Gulch, which fed into it (Brainard 1965:10). By the time he wrote his reminiscence of Humboldt Bay, Brainard was living in New Orleans. He concluded his letter to the *Signal* by indicating that he would never return to Humboldt County, but instead "must content myself with the musical song of the festive alligator, and be lulled to my final slumber by the sweet hum of the mosquito" (Fountain 2001:(56)281).

Brainard's Point proved an obstacle to the development of a shoreside transportation corridor and was first cut through when the C&N was building its rail line between Eureka and Arcata in 1900 and 1901 (Borden 1963:10). The resultant opening was called Brainard's Cut (Turner and Turner 2010:35). When the Redwood Highway was built next to the rail line in the late 1910s, the cut was widened to accommodate the roadway.

Figure 120: The Redwood Highway parallels the NWP's tracks through Brainard's Cut (Humboldt County Public Works).

A report on Brainard's Cut as it was in 1945 was provided by Naida Olsen Gipson, who at the time was a student at Humboldt State College:

> We hit the legal speed limit of about thirty-five miles an hour by the time we entered Branard's [sic] Cut, a high cliff of red-ochre dirt carved with the initials of dare-devils who had had to hang over the edge or climb up the side by sculpting hand- and footholds.
>
> A diner, Ma's Hamburgers, nestled at the base of the cliff. A dirt road wound up the back of the cliff and led to a lovers' lane at the top. but I didn't know about this until years later when my future husband, Ken Gipson, took me there to study the stars (Gipson 2004:29-30).

The Humboldt Bay Oyster Growers Association, Inc. started operating at Brainard in 1933 with a six-acre oyster bed on bay land leased from the NWP. The location was one of seven diked oyster beds on Arcata Bay and the only one on the eastern edge of the bay. The method of using diked beds on tidal flats had been adopted from oyster growers in Puget Sound, Washington. The dikes consisted of low walls made of redwood siding that were held upright by stakes driven into the mud. The tidal flat area was leveled and then "spread with shell and gravel to keep small oysters from sinking into the mud." This method did not work well; the dikes were constructed on poor feeding areas and their walls "obstructed mixing of the water over the beds." The result was "slow growth and poor quality of oysters on diked beds" (Barrett 2020).

Figure 121: Brainard Point 1947, showing *Jupiter* the bay dredge, lower center (HSU Library).

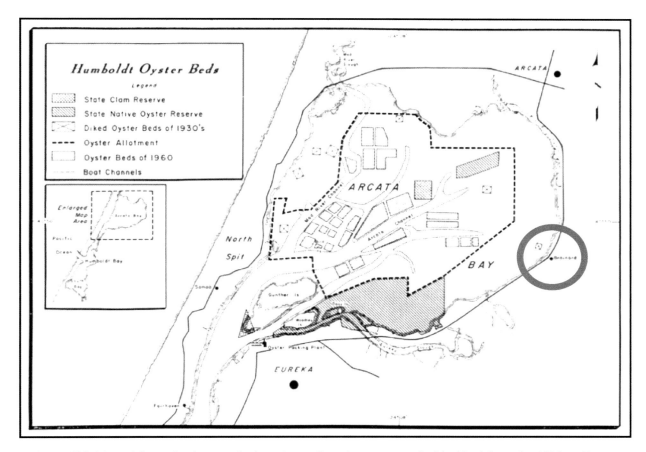

Figure 122: Map of the multiple oyster beds in Arcata Bay, showing a single diked bed from the 1930s at Bracut (Barrett 2020:68).

In 1938 the New England Fish Company established oyster beds at Bird Island in western Arcata Bay, and in 1941 they bought out the Humboldt Bay Oyster Growers Association facility at Brainard Point. The New England Fish Company's tenure there was brief, as they ceased operations in 1943. The oyster allotments for the area were declared abandoned in 1946 (Barrett 2020).

New development came to Brainard's Cut in 1940 when brothers Herb and Glenn Fehely bought the warehouse that had belonged to the New England Fish Company. The brothers, with two other partners, started the Bracut Lumber Company on the site. "Bracut" was coined as a shorten version of Brainard's Cut and the new name came to be applied to the commercial area that evolved in the vicinity of the actual cut. The bay dredge *Jupiter* paid the first of at least three visits in 1947, working next to the fish company's former dock.

For decades the *Jupiter* diligently rearranged parts of Humboldt Bay. She was constructed at the Stockton Iron Works in 1927, built her resumé in central California, and then in the 1940s was towed through the Golden Gate and brought to Humboldt Bay. Her first job was diking in South Bay. She was at Bracut in 1947. In 1949 she restructured the bay shore south of Spruce Point, creating what became King Salmon. Later she went a short distance down the bay and built an addition to the north end of Fields Landing. Later still *Jupiter* again went north into Arcata Bay, dredging at Bra-

Figure 123: January 15, 1947—the bay dredge *Jupiter* works next to the oyster company's former dock. Across the highway, Ma's Hamburgers (serving Coca-Cola) is sandwiched between two parts of Brainard's main business—Auto Wrecking (HSU Library).

Figure 124: *Jupiter*, mired in the mud (HSU Library).

Figure 125: *Jupiter*, R.I.P. (Gisela Rohde).

cut and then working on Arcata's sewage oxidation pond. There, for a time, *Jupiter* stayed. No longer working, she became mired in the mud next to the oxidation pond. In 1963, after being raised from the muck, patched, and otherwise pampered, a resuscitated *Jupiter* spent two more years raising the dikes at the oxidation plant. Next it was back to Bracut for a third visit, this one cut short before the diking was completed. *Jupiter* then returned to South Bay for years of work on the dikes of the Mc-Bride Ranch, coming full circle since the 1940s when teen-aged Andy McBride had been allowed to operate the dredge. Now Andy was on hand to see the aging *Jupiter* in her last years of operation. She finally stopped working in 1987, a sixty-year-old relic whose job was now seen as being detrimental to the environment. The following year the United States Fish and Wildlife Service took over the McBride Ranch and converted it onto a refuge. By then *Jupiter* was reposing on a remnant of White's Slough, visible to bemused motorists passing by on Highway 101. *Jupiter's* owners were ordered to remove her from the wildlife refuge, but they failed to do so. Instead, for the next 14 years she sat in a shallow pond of her own making, enclosed by the dikes she had created when reclamation was still considered an appropriate activity. And then, in July 2002, she burned to the waterline, and suddenly there was one less *Jupiter* in the firmament (Graves 1995; Hodgson 2002).

In 1952 the Bracut Lumber Company applied for a permit from the United States Army Corps of Engineers to create a dike at the Bracut site, mostly north of the former warehouse, that would "create

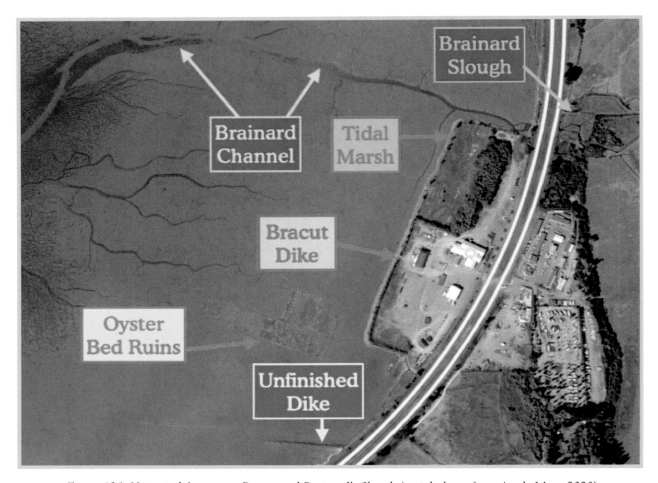

Figure 126: Historical features at Bracut and Brainard's Slough (aerial photo from Apple Maps 2020).

a nearly 225-acre property" The actual diked area turned out to be only about 32 acres (Miller and Mc-
Morris 2014:17). The "low hill" that was then the western portion of Brainard's Point was leveled and
the soil used to fill an adjacent section of bay flats. In mid-July *Jupiter* was busy "building a dike from bay
mud to protect the filled sections of the property." A planing mill and dry kiln, belonging to a company
accurately but unimaginatively named Humboldt Dry Kiln, were being built on the site, which was just
north of the Bracut Lumber Company. The new operation was expected to "turn out 200,000 board
feet of lumber per week." Humboldt Dry Kiln was associated with the Arcata Lumber Company (Arcata Union, July 18, 1952; Miller and McMorris 2014:17). In October 1955 a fire destroyed the mill and
its lumber at Humboldt Dry Kiln, a loss of about $200,000 (Blue Lake Advocate, October 20, 1955).

That same year the Bracut Lumber Company was purchased by John H. Hess, Ben Schindler,
and Ken Startup. The new owners used the site "for loading lumber for the Simonson Lumber Company of Smith River, in Del Norte County. In 1959 the Simonsen sales office was moved to Bracut"
(Miller and McMorris 2014:17).

Figure 127: Photo showing former oyster beds (cerise arrow) and uncompleted southern dike (tan arrow) (Humboldt County Public Works).

VI. The Legacy of Landform Transformation

By 2020 the eastern edge of Arcata Bay had experienced 170 years of alterations made by the early white arrivals and their successors. The bay shore and the sloughs were lined with dikes and causeways, while thousands of acres of wetlands had been transformed into ranchlands and business sites. The shape of the bay shore had changed at Bracut and Brainard, where portions of the bay had been diked and filled to accommodate expanding commercial interests. Planes, trains, and cars and trucks traveled on former marshlands that had been dedicated to the various vehicles' use. The completely natural environment of 1850 became a highly specialized, artificial environment by 2020, an environment that, unlike its predecessor, did not tend to itself.

The North Coast Railroad Authority, successor to the NWP, has not performed any significant maintenance of the railroad around Humboldt Bay for nearly two decades. Storm events combined with daily tidal action continue to take a toll on the integrity and stability of the railbed. While CalTrans and Humboldt County take care of parts of the area's infrastructure, no agency has had the responsibility for maintaining the water barriers that have defined the lowlands east of the bay. Ranchers and other property owners strive to repair the dikes that keep most of the land from flooding, but there is no comprehensive plan in place to address the oncoming effects of sea level rise. The prospects of managing such a large landscape (and seascape) spanning multiple ownerships in the modern age of laws and regulations are immensely challenging.

While this report has focused on the history of the land east of Arcata Bay, a brief review of the current condition of various historical features can help inform future planning for certain changes that will address the effects of Sea Level Rise. Work done by Aldaron Laird and others has provided detailed information about the artificial features of the area, some of which are displayed here.

A. Northeast Arcata Bay

The entire shoreline of northeastern Arcata Bay is artificial. Water flow is controlled by seven tide gates between Gannon Slough and Brainard. Most of the shoreline is armored by the aging NWP rail line causeway, which was completed in 1900. The shoreline at Brainard was diked by 1898, with expansion diking done in the 1950s and 1960. Part of the shoreline was diked at Bracut starting in 1952. Smaller dike units are in place at Jacoby Creek and Gannon Slough. These date from Harpst and Spring's work in 1892. Part of Bracut is bounded by fill.

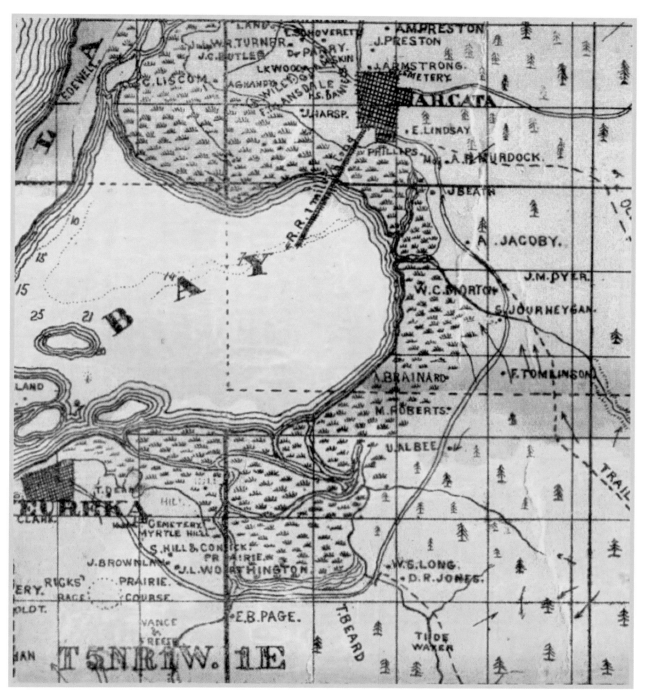

Figure 128: Arcata Bay, 1865, with wetlands intact (Doolittle 1865).

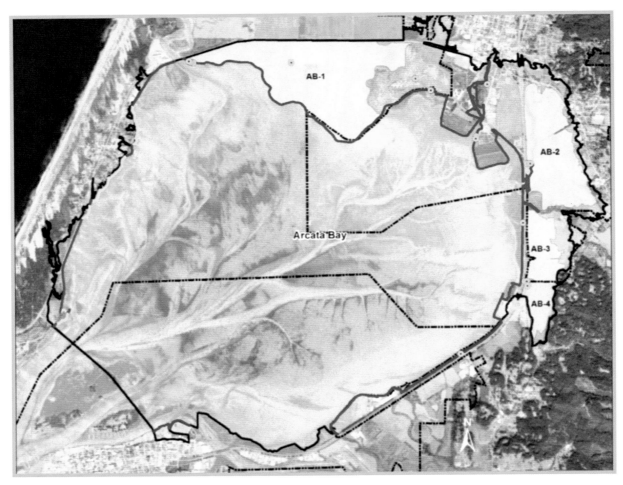

Figure 129: Arcata Bay shoreline, 2020, showing diked units in light blue, artificial shoreline in dark blue, and tide gates as yellow circles (Trinity Associates 2020).

Figure 130: Railbed remnant at the mouth of Brainard Slough (Humboldt County Public Works).

Figure 131: Flooding from Gannon Slough (Aldaron Laird)

Figure 132: Mouth of Gannon Slough (Aldaron Laird).

Figure 133: Brainard Slough remnant (Aldaron Laird).

Figure 134: Bayside Cutoff (at left) and Brainard Slough (at right) (Humboldt County Public Works).

Figure 135: Jacoby Creek, east of Highway 101 (Aldaron Laird).

B. The Eureka Slough Complex

Most of the shorelines in the Eureka slough complex are artificial. The main areas with natural shorelines are: 1) on Second and Third sloughs, 2) near the south end of Walker Point, and 3) the eastern end of Freshwater Slough. There are 16 tide gates in the diked system. The C&N rail line causeway, completed in 1901, serves as a dike from the southwest end of Brainard to near the mouth of Eureka Slough. Gross and Sinclair, who owned much of the land in the slough system, finished diking in 1896. The Pacific Lumber Company railroad causeway adjacent today's Murray Field was completed in 1906.

Two small areas have reverted to wetlands. In March 2011 a section of the upper Fay Slough dike was overtopped, flooding a 16-acre area. That May, the California Department of Fish and Wildlife and the Redwood Community Action Agency breached the dike in two places to allow the flooded area to drain. However, "the breaches were dug deep enough that ebbing tides can keep the breach channel open. This has allowed the area to be restored to an inter-tidal wetland state of mudflat and marsh" (Laird 2020a). Near the eastern end of Park Street, the Freshwater Slough dike was breached by the Humboldt Bay Harbor and Recreation District. The breach has created an inter-tidal wetland on the site of a former log pond; it serves as mitigation "for the wetlands impacts from constructing the Woodley Island Marina" (Laird 2020a).

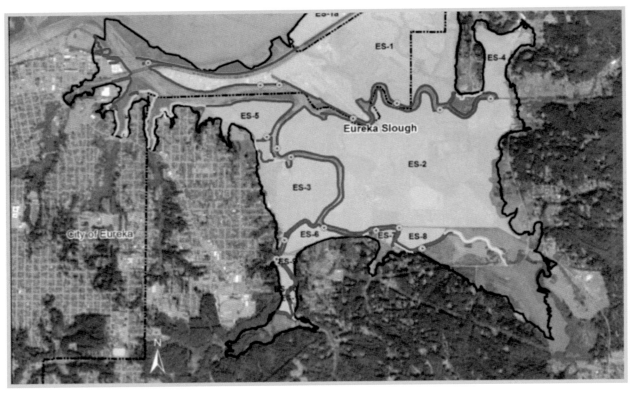

Figure 136: Southeastern Arcata Bay 2020 shoreline, with diked units in light blue, artificial shoreline in dark blue, undiked sloughs in yellow, and tide gates as yellow circles (Trinity Associates 2020).

Figure 137: Railbed causeway serving as a dike at Indianola Cutoff (Humboldt County Public Works).

Figure 138: Northeastern portion of former Devoy Ranch and truncated slough (Humboldt County Public Works).

Figure 139: The north end of the Brainard dike (Humboldt County Public Works).

Figure 140: King Tide at Brainard (Aldaron Laird).

Figure 141 Eureka Slough, with businesses on Jacobs Avenue (Humboldt County Public Works)

Figure 142: The north bank of Eureka Slough shows both armored and unarmored areas (Aldaron Laird).

Figure 143: North bank of Eureka Slough with unarmored section on right (Aldaron Laird).

Figure 144: North bank of Eureka Slough, heavily armored (Aldaron Laird).

Figure 145: Reversed reclamation: returned wetland, center, southwest of Walker Point (Humboldt County Public Works).

Figure 146: Induced breach of Fay Slough, 2013 (Aldaron Laird).

Figure 147: Heavily vegetated dike bank on Fay Slough (Aldaron Laird).

Figure 148: Sparsely vegetated dike bank on Fay Slough (Aldaron Laird).

Figure 149: Undiked slough bank, upper Freshwater Slough (Aldaron Laird)

Figure 150: Freshwater Slough gets close to Myrtle Avenue during a king tide (Aldaron Laird).

Figure 151: Green boat close at hand, this Freshwater Slough residence appears ready for sea level rise. But what will happen to Myrtle Avenue, where the silver car travels in the background? (Aldaron Laird).

Figure 152: Eroding Freshwater Slough bank next to former McKay & Co. railbed (Aldaron Laird).

Figure 153: Egrets on lower Freshwater Slough dike; radio towers in background, upper right (Aldaron Laird).

Figure 154: Returned wetland off Freshwater Slough next to former McKay & Co. log dump (Humboldt County Public Works).

Sources

Barrett, Elinore M.

    2020 The California Oyster Industry. Web page. Electronic Document, https://oac.cdlib.org/view?docId=kt629004n3&brand=oac4&doc.view=entire_text accessed on April 7, 2020.

Bay Journal

    2020a Selwyn Eddy (1847-1911). Web page. Electronic Document, http://bay-journal.com/bay/1he/writings/eddy-selwyn-1911.html accessed on March 17, 2020.

Belcher Abstract & Title Co.

    1921-1922 Atlas of Humboldt County, California. Eureka: Belcher Abstract & Title Co.

Belcher and Crane

    1916 Street and Guide Map of the City of Eureka, Humboldt County, California. Eureka: Belcher and Crane Company.

Bledsoe, A. J.

    1885 Indian Wars of the Northwest. San Francisco: Bacon & Co.

Blow, Ben

    1920 California Highways. San Francisco: H. S. Crocker.

Borden, Stanley

    1949a The Pacific Lumber Co. The Western Railroader 12(8).

    1954a Arcata & Mad River. The Western Railroader 17(8).

    1958a Oregon & Eureka Railroad. The western Railroader 22(1).

    1961a The Great Railroad Fight. Humboldt County Historical Society Newsletter, September 1961.

    1963a San Francisco & Northwestern. The western Railroader 26(1).

Bowcutt, Frederica

    2015 The Tanoak Tree. Seattle: University of Washington Press.

Brainard, W. A.

    1965 A California Reminiscence. Humboldt County Historical Society Newsletter, May-June 1965.

Bridgehunter.com

    2020a Eureka Slough Bridge. Web page. Electronic document, https://bridgehunter.com/ca/humboldt/40022l/ accessed on April 15, 2020.

cahighways.org

    2020 California Highways Routes 97 through 104. Web page. Electronic document, https://www.cahighways.org/097-104.html#101 accessed on April 5, 2020.

California Bricks

    2009a John B. Hill. In California Bricks. Web Page. Electronic document, https://calbricks.netfirms.com/brick.hilljohnb.html accessed on March 27, 2020.

    2009b Eureka Brick & Tile Company, Thompson Brick & Tile Company, J. D. Thompson Brick

Company. *In* California Bricks. Web Page. Electronic document, https://calbricks.netfirms.com/brick.eurekabm.html accessed on March 27, 2020.

2009c Humboldt Clay Manufacturing Company. *In* California Bricks. Web Page. Electronic document, https://calbricks.netfirms.com/brick.humboldt.html accessed on March 27, 2020.

California Highway Commission

1922   Second Biennial Report.

California Highways and Public Works

1947   Legislation Provides $76,000,000 Annually for New Construction on California State Highway System, Illustrated. California Highways and Public Works (26)7,8.

1953   Burns Freeway. California Highways and Public Works (32)9-10).

California State Supreme Court

1906   Reports of Cases Determined in the Supreme Court of the State of California, vol. 94. San Francisco: Bancroft-Whitney Company.

Call, Ryan

2020   From Recycling to Reducing: A Brief History of Waste Management in Humboldt County. Web page. Electronic document, https://www.yournec.org/from-recyling-to-reducing-a-brief-history-of-waste-management-in-humboldt-county/ accessed on April 8, 2020.

Canter, Adam

2020 Personal communication with Jerry Rohde, June 10, 2020.

carljohnsonco.com

2020. The Carl Johnson Company: History. Web page. Electronic Document, https://www.carljohnsonco.com/ourhistory accessed on April 10, 2020.

Carranco, Lynwood

1982   Redwood Lumber Industry. San Marino, California: Golden West Books.

Carranco, Lynwood, and Henry L. Sorensen

1988   Steam in the Redwoods. Caldwell, Idaho: The Caxton Printers, Ltd.

Casetext

2020   Sacchi v. Bayside Lumber Co. Web page. Electronic document, https://casetext.com/case/sacchi-v-bayside-lumber-co accessed on July 12, 2020.

Cerny, Frank J.

2007   Interview with Green Diamond Forester Greg Templeton. Photocopy in author's files.

Cinema Treasures

2020   Midway Drive-In. Web page. Electronic document, http://cinematreasures.org/theaters/15106 accessed on March 31, 2020.

Cole, Cedar

1984   Freshwater Corners: Crossroads of Time. Photocopy in author's possession.

County of Humboldt, Department of Public Works

2020   Comment Evaluation Memo, Humboldt Bay Trail South Web page. Electronic Document, https://humboldtgov.org/DocumentCenter/View/64362/CEQA-Comment-Evaluation-Memo accessed on April 27, 2020.

Coy, Owen C.
    1982[1929] The Humboldt Bay Region 1850 – 1875. Eureka: Humboldt County Historical Society.

Curtis, Edward S.
    1970[1924] The North American Indian, volume 13. New York: Johnson Reprint Corporation.

Davis, Olive
    1977 Spear Family Tree and History. Partial photocopy in author's possession.

Deitrich, Waldemar Fenn
    1928 The Clay Resources and the Ceramic Industry of California. Division of Mines and Mining
    Bulletin No. 99. San Francisco: Division of Mines and Mining.

Denny, Edward
    1911 Denny's Official Map of the County of Humboldt California. San Francisco: Edward Denny &
    Co.

Dillon, Kathy
    2008 A Changing Landscape. Times-Standard, November 16, 2008.

Doolittle, A. J.
    1865 Official Township Map of Humboldt Co., Cal. San Francisco: A. J. Doolittle.

Doran, Bob
    2006 Mudflat Confessions. North Coast Journal, May 25, 2006.

Driver, Harold E.
    1939 Cultural Element Distributions: X Northwestern California. Anthropological Records (1)6.

Eddy, J. M.
    1893 In the Redwoods Realm. San Francisco: D. M. Stanley & Co.

Evans, Barry
    2020a Personal communication with Jerry Rhode, April 16, 2020.

Farmer, Ruth McCabe
    2014 Interview with Jerry Rohde.

Forbes, Stanly
    1886 Official Map of Humboldt County, California. San Francisco: Stanly Forbes.

Fountain, Susie Baker
    2001 Susie Baker Fountain Papers. 128 volumes. Microfilm: Humboldt State University Library, Arca-
    ta.

Genzoli, Andrew
    1973 Redwood Country . . . Legacy of the Pioneer. Eureka: Schooner Features.

Gipson, Naida Olsen
    2004 The Girls of '45. Humboldt Historian, Fall 2004.

Golla, Victor
    2011 California Indian Languages. Berkeley: University of California Press.

Graves, Wally
    1995 Bankrupt on Jupiter. North Coast Journal, May 1995.

Hamm, Lillie E.
    1890 History and Business Directory of Humboldt County. Eureka: Daily Humboldt Standard.

Hart, Alan S.

1955 Burns Freeway. California Highways and Public Works, Sept-Oct 1955.

Hedlund, Eric

1978 An Historic Resources Inventory: The Old Arcata Road-Myrtle Avenue Corridor. Eureka: Natural Resources Division, Humboldt County Department of Public Works.

Hewes, Gordon W.

1940 Wiyot Notes. Photocopy in possession of author.

Hilfiker, Bill

2015 Harold Otto Hilfiker: Humboldt's Premier Pipe Maker. Humboldt Historian, fall 2015.

Hindley, Lorine, and Karl Klingenspor

2009 Phone interview with Jerry Rohde, July 1, 2009.

Hodgson, Judy

2002 Final Chapters. North Coast Journal, July 11, 2002.

Hunt, Chris

1998 Island of Tears. Times-Standard, March 15, 1998.

Irvine, Leigh H.

1915 History of Humboldt County, California. Los Angeles: Historic Record Co.

Jewett, W. H.

1964 Memories of Old Humboldt. Humboldt Historical Society Newsletter, May-June 1964.

JRP Historical Consulting Services

2004 Route 101 Eureka-Arcata Corridor Highway Improvement Project: Historic Resources Evaluation Report. Davis, California: JRP Historical Consulting Services.

Kneiss, Gilbert

1956 Redwood Railways. Berkeley: Howell North.

Laird, Aldaron

2005 Applying the Public Trust Doctrine to Humboldt Bay. Copy in possession of author.

2020a Personal communication with the author, April 30, 2020.

Lentell, J. N.

1898 Official Map of Humboldt County California. N. p.

Lewis, Oscar, ed.

1966 The Quest for Qual-a-wa-loo. Oakland: Holmes Book Company.

Lowell, F. A.

1915 Mines and Mineral Resources of Del Norte County Humboldt County Mendocino County. California State Mining Bureau: California State Printing Office.

Magno, Maria, and Jane Monroe

2020 Camas. Web page. Electronic document, https://tommendenhall.com/ethnobotany/ethnobotany.php accessed on June 7, 2020.

measuringworth.com

2020a Income value of $41,500 in 1920 dollars today. Web page. Electronic document, https://www.measuringworth.com/dollarvaluetoday/?amount=41500&from=1920 accessed on July 12, 2020.

2020b Inflated worth of $3,500 in 1907 dollars today. Web page. Electronic document, https://www.measuringworth.com/dollarvaluetoday/?amount=3500&from=1907 accessed on July 12, 2020.

Metsker, Charles F.

1949 Metsker's Atlas of Humboldt County, California. Tacoma, WA: Charles F. Metsker.

Miller, Heather, and Christopher McMorris

2014 Historical Resources Evaluation Report: Phase II Arcata Rail with Trail Connectivity Project, City of Arcata, Humboldt County, California. Davis, California: JPR Historical Consulting, LLC.

2018 Historical Resources Evaluation Report: Humboldt Bay South Project, Humboldt County, California. Davis, California: JPR Historical Consulting, LLC.

Mitchell, Daniel J. B.

2020 How California Created a Roadmap for America's Interstate System. Web page. Electronic document, https://issuu.com/danieljbmitchell/docs/how_california_created_a_road_map_f accessed on April 5, 2020.

Mitchell, Sean

2020 The Demise of the Northwestern Pacific Railroad. Web page. Electronic document, http://humboldt-dspace.calstate.edu/bitstream/handle/10211.3/131780/Mitchell_Sean_Barnum_f.pdf?sequence=1 accessed on March 29, 2020.

Moore, Rusty

2020 Phone interview with Jerry Rohde, June 5, 2020.

Nash, Glen

1996 Making a Living, Making a Life in Humboldt County. Eureka: Eureka Printing Company.

National Coopers' Journal

1907a Editorial Notes. National Coopers' Journal, May 1907.

NWP

1916 Right of Way and Track Map: Korblex Branch, Eureka to Korblex. San Francisco: Office of Chief Engineer Maintenance.

1917 [Map of] Brainard and Bayside, Humboldt County.

onevoter.org

2020 Assembly Districts 1941. Web page. Electronic document, http://www.onevoter.org/wp-content/uploads/sites/4/2015/08/1941AD.jpg accessed on April 10, 2020.

Pettengill, Bert

1961 Freshwater Corners. Humboldt County Historical Society Newsletter, November 1961.

Philipsen, Richard

2014a Interview with Jerry Rohde, January 27, 2014.

Polk-Husted

1913 Eureka City and Humboldt County Directory 1913. Sacramento: Polk-Husted Directory Company.

Renzullo, Jennifer

2009 Brickyard site inspection interview with Jerry Rohde, June 19, 2009.

Roberts, Earl

1972 Bayside Mill. Humboldt Historian, March-April 1972, (20)2:4.

Robinson, W. W.

1948 Land in California. Berkeley: University of California Press.

Rohde, Gisela

1995 Field notes for botanizing trip to Kneeland and Showers Pass, May 14, 1995. Original in possession of author.

Rohde, Jerry

2014a McKay Tract Community Forest: Regaining the Valley of the Giants.

2014b Both Sides of the Bluff. Eureka: MountainHome Books.

2020a The Sonoma Gang. Web page. Electronic document, https://www.northcoastjournal.com/humboldt/the-sonoma-gang/Content?oid=2127928 accessed on April 12, 2020.

2020b Genocide and Extortion. Web page. Electronic document, https://www.northcoastjournal.com/humboldt/genocide-and-extortion/Content?oid=2130748 accessed on April 13, 2020.

N.d. Comments from an unidentified member of the audience at a presentation given by the author.

Forthcoming Southern Humboldt Hinterlands. Eureka: MountainHome Books.

Rohde, Jerry, and Jim Timmons

2016 Feeding the Hungriest Humboldters. Humboldt Historian, Summer 2016:26-33.

Roscoe, James

1997 Final Report of a Cultural Resources Data Recovery and Monitoring Program at the Price-Costco Site, Eureka, California. Submitted to SHN, Consulting Engineers and Geologist, Eureka, California. Copy available at the Cultural Resources Facility, Humboldt State University.

Roscoe, Neb

1995 Transporting Shingles from Pinkerton's Mill. Humboldt Historian, Winter 1995:14-15).

Sanborn Map Company

1920 Insurance Maps Eureka California. New York, New York: Sanborn Map Company.

1957 Insurance Maps of Eureka California Including Fairhaven & Samoa. New York, New York: Sanborn Map Company.

Schafran, Walter

1984 Bayside Through the Years. Center for Community Development, Humboldt State University.

Shoe & Leather Reporter

1919 Annual. Boston: The Shoe & Leather Reporter Co.

Sommer, Bob

2006 Not So Kinetic: A look back at Humboldt's mudflat sculpture gallery. North Coast Journal, May 25, 2006.

Spear Memorial Foundation

N.d. Untitled document pertaining to the Spear cousins and the Indian Island Massacre. Eureka: The Matilda & Nancy Spear Memorial Foundation.

State of California, Division of Highways

1928 Sixth Biennial Report.

State of California, California Highway Commission

1922 First Biennial Report.

State of California, Office of Historic Preservation

2006 Letter of comment to Department of Transportation re: Eureka-Arcata Corridor projects, November 29, 2006.

Stindt, Fred A., and Guy L. Dunscomb

1964 The Northwestern Pacific Railroad. N. p.

Streamline Planning Consultants

2015 Preliminary Surveying Analysis of Railroad Right-of-Way. Arcata: Streamline Planning Consultants.

Templeton, Greg

2020 Phone interview with Jerry Rohde, April 13, 2020.

Times Publishing Co.

1902 Souvenir of Humboldt County. Eureka: Times Publishing Co.

Turner, Dennis W. and Gloria H. Turner

2010 Place Names of Humboldt County, 2nd Ed. California. Orangevale, CA: Dennis W. & Gloria H. Turner.

U. S. Surveyor General's Office

1855a Township N° 5 North, Range N° 1 East, Humboldt Meridian. San Francisco: U. S. Surveyor General's Office.

1890a Township N° 5 North, Range N° 1 East, Humboldt Meridian. San Francisco: U. S. Surveyor General's Office.

United States Army Corps of Engineers

1922. Controlled Reconnaissance Sheet 9 – N – II - E/2.

United States Coast Survey

1870 Part of Humboldt Bay, California.

1916 Humboldt Bay, California.

1957 Humboldt Bay, California.

United States Department of Agriculture, Bureau of Soils

1921 Soil Map, California, Eureka Sheet.

USGS

1933 Eureka Quadrangle. United States Department of the Interior, U.S. Geological Survey.

1942 Eureka Quadrangle. United States Department of the Interior, U.S. Geological Survey.

1951 Eureka Quadrangle. United States Department of the Interior, U.S. Geological Survey.

1972 Arcata South Quadrangle. United States Department of the Interior, U.S. Geological Survey.

Van Kirk, Susie

2006a Fay Slough References for "Fay Slough Tributaries Enhancement Project." Electronic copy in author's possession.

2006b Freshwater Slough Histories. Report for the Northcoast Regional Land Trust and Redwood Community Action Agency.

2006c Research Notes Freshwater Slough and Fay Slough. Electronic copy in author's possession.

2007a Fay Slough Tributaries Enhancement Project. Report for the Redwood Community Action Agency, Eureka, California.

2015a Arcata Marsh History: Union Wharf, Mad River Canal, Reclamation, Lumber Mills, City Design. Copy in author's possession.

2020a Northwestern Pacific Railroad. Web page. Electronic document, https://en.wikipedia.org/wiki/Northwestern_Pacific_Railroad accessed on March 29, 2020.

wildlife.ca.gov

2020 Fay Slough Wildlife Area. Web page. Electronic document, https://wildlife.ca.gov/Lands/Places-to-Visit/Fay-Slough-WA#11018143-history accessed on April 6, 2020.

Wikimedia Commons

2020a File: Midway Drive-In Screen Indianola CA. Web page. Electronic document, https://commons.wikimedia.org/wiki/File:Midway_Drive-In_Screen_Indianola_CA.JPG accessed on March 31, 2020.

List of Figures

Figure 42: Harpst & Spring Shingle Mill at the future site of Sunny Brae (HSU Library).

Figure 43: The ferry *Antelope* at play on Humboldt Bay (HSU Library).

Figure 44: Northern end of HLRR shown in pink. Later Pacific Lumber Company Railroad extension shown in green (Cole 1984).

Figure 45: Excelsior Redwood Company trains near Freshwater Corners, c. 1891, showing three trains of logs and one (far right) with rock for the Humboldt Bay jetties (Jack Irvine Collection).

Figure 46: Yellow arrow points to remnant of Freshwater Landing, south of Murray Field; cerise arrow points to Pacific Lumber Company Railroad grade (Humboldt County Public Works).

Figure 47: An 1898 map showing the E&F's rail line ending at Freshwater Landing (Lentell 1898).

Figure 48: Northern end of the Pacific Lumber Company Railroad and other nearby features (aerial photo from Apple Maps 2020).

Figure 49: While auto traffic waits, a Pacific Lumber Company engine hauls empties crosses Highway 101 in 1940. Steam from the engine is visible to the right of the Murray Field hangar (Humboldt County Public Works).

Figure 50: No longer needed. Abandoned water tank next to abandoned rails at Eddyville (author's collection).

Figure 51: Pacific Lumber Company Railroad causeway, center, between Murray Field, left, and the Farm Store, right (Jerry Rohde).

Figure 52: FB&C log dump on Gannon Slough (HSU Library).

Figure 53: The bounty of Bayside: logs (left) and shingles (right), probably at Gannon Slough, c. 1910 (HSU Library).

Figure 54: Flanigan, Brosnan and Company's Shingle Wharf, looking east. Shingles line the wharf, while rock from the company's quarry is being towed by the tugboat (HSU Library).

Figure 55: Flanigan, Brosnan and Company's wharf piling adjacent the oxidation pond (Jerry Rohde).

Fugure 56: Twenty-one carloads of Jacoby Creek Quarry rock arrive at the unloading apron on the South Spit (HSU Library).

Figure 57: Route of FB&C rail line northwest of Bayside (aerial photo from Apple Maps 2020).

Figure 58: In 1922 the McKay and Co. railroad (orange) ran north to their log dump and shingle mill on Freshwater Slough. The Pacific Lumber Company Railroad (purple) went north to Freshwater Junction, where it connected with the Northwestern Pacific Railroad (pink). The Eureka-Arcata road (green) crossed the wetlands west of Freshwater Corners (Belcher Abstract & Title Co.)

Figure 59: McKay & Co. shingle mill, Freshwater Slough (HSU Library).

Figure 60: McKay & Co. log dump on Freshwater Slough, north of Park Street (Aldaron Laird).

Figure 61: McKay & Co. #1 near the Freshwater Slough log dump (Humboldt County Historical Society).

Figure 62; The Occidental Mill used part of Humboldt Bay for its log pond (thehumboldtproject.org).

Figure 85: Lift-span state highway bridge over Eureka Slough, c. 1920 (State of California Highway Commission 1922:146).

Figure 86: A 1948 photo of the truncated Parker truss bridge (cerise arrow) that replaced the original lift span bridge for the highway crossing over Eureka Slough (HSU Library).

Figure 87: Traffic crowds Highway 101 on Arcata's G Street in the early 1950s (California Highways and Public Works 1953:2).

Figure 88: Southern end of the Michael J. Burns Freeway, 1957, showing the four-lane roadway, two freeway bridges, the NWP pivot bridge, and business development along Jacobs Avenue (HSU Library).

Figure 89: An 1890 revision of General Land Office map showing what had previously been labeled "Salt Marsh" as "Swamp & Overflowed Land" in township 5N, 1E, Humboldt Meridian. The change in terminology was necessary to allow the state to sell these lands, at a nominal price, rather having them retained as state sovereign lands (U. S. Surveyor General's Office 1890a).

Figure 90: Arcata-Jacoby Creek diking machine, 1893 (HSU Library).

Figure 91: "Break in levee . . . looking towards Sunny Brae near Bayside. . . " (HSU Library).

Figure 92: Court exhibit in Sacchi vs. Bayside Lumber Co. showing material in upper Jacoby Creek (Jack Irvine Collection).

Figure 93: Court exhibit in Sacchi vs. Bayside Lumber Co. showing logging debris in upper Jacoby Creek (Jack Irvine Collection).

Figure 94: Devoy Ranch, west of Freshwater Slough, 1901. Walker Point in distance, right (Times Publishing Co. 1902:93).

Figure 95: Wheat threshing, probably on Freshwater Investment Company farmland, c. 1910 (author's collection).

Figure 96: Drawbridge over Freshwater Slough near Myrtle Avenue (HSU Library).

Figure 97: Fay Slough Wildlife Area vs. H. M. Devoy Ranch.

Figure 98: The Dragon (North Coast Journal)

Figure 99: Pressed brick from Eureka Brick & Tile Company (California Bricks).

Figure 100: J. D. Thompson Brick Company (Deitrich 1928).

Figure 101: J. D. Thompson Brick & Tile Company brickworks (note the hollow tiles in front of the water tank), looking west down Eureka Slough (HSU Library).

Figure 102: Brickyard sites on lower Eureka Slough, with Park Street in foreground, Jacobs Avenue in background, 1954 (HSU Library).

Figure 103: Former office, Hindley Clay Products (Jerry Rohde).

Figure 104: Lower Eureka Slough area, 1937, showing dike along northern side of slough (purple arrow) that protects the future site of Jacobs Avenue, and the undiked area north of Highway 101 (green arrow) that remains wetland (Humboldt County Public Works)

Appendix: Rail Line Rights-of-Way Deed and Authorization Inventory

Segment 1 – East Eureka to Eureka Slough

CNR purchased a roughly triangular piece of land from Tydd in April, 1900 (#211, 69 Deeds 610) adjacent to Eureka Slough. They then purchased an irregular piece from Eureka & Freshwater Railway in August, 1901 (#210, 71 Deeds 541) from #211 to V Street.

NWP purchased back portions of the previous CNR properties above from Williamson in September, 1964 ("F", 806 O.R. 313) from Y Street to the Eureka Slough. Further research could provide the details of what transpired, but not necessary at this time.

Segment 2 – Eureka Slough to Fay Slough

CNR purchased a 66-foot-wide strip of land from F.E. Herrick in June, 1900 (#215, 71 Deeds 590) from the east bank of Eureka Slough to the west bank of a slough in the center of the NW¼ of the NW¼ of Section 19 (Fay Slough). In 1901, CNR also purchased a large parcel of land from Herrick, adjacent and north of the tracks (#216, 76 Deeds 314). This land (#216) is no longer owned by the railroad.

EKR received permission to construct its line over two separate areas of state lands in July, 1899 (#217, LRA 177). This permission included survey bearings and there is also an accompanying map showing the approved locations, one from Arcata to Bracut and the second from Eureka to a line labelled "Two Mile Limit" near Fay Slough. Shuster photos from the 1940s show roadbed and it's [sic] possible tracks were built this far towards Eureka, although the line was never completed. This study was unable to determine the precise end of construction towards Eureka, and found no evidence of an EKR bridge over Eureka Slough ever being constructed.

*Spatial relation note: There is a minute difference between the CNR and EKR in the bearing of the straight course leading to Eureka Slough. This either implies disregard by Herrick of EKR's permit location (why not just make them parallel to each other?) or they are indeed parallel and Herrick uses a different basis of bearing than Lentell. Interesting historically, but not really affecting this study, as the CNR won out and both were ultimately absorbed by NWP.

Segment 3 – Fay Slough to Indianola Cutoff

CNR purchased a 66-foot-wide right-of-way for railroad purposes from Gross & Sinclair in July, 1900 (#218, 70 Deeds 364) from a point on the north side of the centerline of Section 17 (Indianola Cutoff) to "the bank of a slough in the middle of the NW¼ of the NW¼ of Section 19" (Fay Slough). This could be a reference to the west bank as called out in Herrick's deed, or it could be the east bank, in which case there would be a slight gap. This study finds at least two pieces of evidence supporting the west bank: 1) the distances in the deed descriptions are approximately correct when fit to the GHD survey of the existing tracks to support the ends of the two deeds matching up on the west bank; and 2) the NWP tracks maps show no gap at the slough (although they do show the segments meeting in the center of the slough rather than the west bank).

EKR purchased a 60-foot-wide railroad right-of-way from C. Hooper in April, 1899 (#219, 65 Deeds 488). This deed contains references to other deeds that are necessary to define exactly what the nature of these are or any agreements that go along with them. According to this deed, Hooper is merely selling his railroad rights as reserved by Davis & Bates when they sold the land to Gross in July, 1891, which rights Davis & Bates then had sold to Hooper in November, 1891 (recorded March, 1899 in 65 Deeds 457). Again, what could be a roadbed is visible in the Shuster photos of the late 1940's, adjacent and west of the CNR tracks.

Segment 4 – Bracut

CNR purchased a variable width strip of land from G. Pinkerton in July, 1900 (#220, 70 Deeds 366) from a point on the north side of the centerline of Section 17 (Indianola Cutoff) to the north line of the SW¼ of Section 9 (north edge of Bracut).

EKR purchased a variable with strip of land from G. Pinkerton in May, 1899 (#221, 66 Deeds 419) from a point on the north side of the centerline of Section 17 (Indianola Cutoff) to the south line of fractional SE¼ of Section 8 (north edge of Bracut).

These parcels were omitted in the transfer from NWP to Eureka Southern in 1984 (NWP granted them an easement instead). NWP then sold the underlying fee title to Bracut Lumber in May, 1986.

Segment 5 – Bayside

After initiating condemnation proceedings in superior court, CNR won a judgment in March, 1902 (#268, Case 3850) for railroad purposes over the SE corner of Section 8 (NE Bracut). They purchased a 132-foot-wide wide by 660-foot-long piece of land in September, 1902 (#224, 84 Deeds 610) adjacent to the east line of their existing right-of-way from Bayside cutoff going south (this study finds no existing CNR right-of-way over this portion in 1902). Carson granted a right of way to CNR in December, 1902 (#225, 82 Deeds 431) from the south line of the NW¼ of the NW¼ of Section 9 to the north line of the SW¼ of the SW¼ of Section 4, recorded in May, 1903. There seems to be some unnecessary overlap here between the Carson and Smith deeds. One theory that this study can posit is that #225 is the right-of-way referred to in #224, and that the property description of #225 is incorrect and should have described the NW¼ of Section 9 rather than the NW¼ of the NW¼ of Section 9 and the SW¼ of the SW¼ of Section 4. Further evidence which supports this theory is that CNR had already acquired fee title over the SW¼ of the SW¼ of Section 4 from John Smith in June, 1900 (#226, 72 Deeds 443). Further research in this regard would specify which properties Carson and Smith owned in that area between 1900 and 1903 (specifically if Carson had purchased the SW¼ of the SW¼ of Section 4 sometime after #226 was granted and before #225 was granted).

NWP cleaned up any potential ambiguity in 1917 with acquisitions from Roberts (#222, 137 Deeds 377) and Carson (#223, 139 Deeds 83) over the SW¼ of the NW¼ of Section 9. In December 1917, NWP granted #224 (and other small unnecessary properties adjacent to the east side of the corridor) to the State of California.

The important thing to take away from this progression is that after April 1917, #222, #223, & #226 made a 66-foot-wide fee corridor from the north side of Bracut to just south of the Jacoby Creek crossing.

EKR's permission over this Segment from the state was described in Segment 2.

Segment 6 – Jacoby Creek/Gannon Slough

CNR purchased a 66-foot-wide right-of-way for railroad purposes from Flanigan et. al. in June, 1900 (#228 & #229, 70 Deeds 445) from the one eighth section line 1,479 feet south and 179.4 in relation to the section line would be a beneficial supplement to this study. In any event, it appears clear that the intention of all parties in 1900 was for the railroad to be adjacent to the section line. This "Bayside" Segment represents the end of project just as the tracks turn westerly into South G Street in Arcata.

A potential inconsistency was noted with respect to the legal descriptions within the deeds for the right-of-way along the west side of Section 4. The NWP Bracut Station Map V-4 / S12a appears to have the best depiction of how the corridor is supposed to fit the section line. If one holds the NWP mapping to be a correct depiction, then the issue arises with the Flanigan deed, which does not align adjacent to the west line of Section 4 like all the deeds leading up to it. Alternatively, if the Flanigan deed is the one positioned correctly away from the line, then the corridor from south of Flanigan back down to Bracut could potentially be outside of its deeded right-of-way. A survey locating the west line of Sections 9 and 4 to identify where the tracks lie in relation to the section line would be a beneficial supplement to this study. In any event, it appears clear that the intention of all parties in 1900 was for the railroad to be adjacent to the section line.

This "Bayside" Segment represents the end of project just as the tracks turn westerly into South G Street in Arcata.

EKR permission over this Segment was described in Segment 2.

(Source for entire appendix: Streamline Planning Consultants 2015:7-10.)

Made in the USA
Middletown, DE
15 January 2022

58742514R00095